Grant Writing with AI

by Sheryl Lindsell-Roberts, MA

for
dúmmies®
A Wiley Brand

Grant Writing with AI For Dummies®

Published by: **John Wiley & Sons, Inc.**, 111 River Street, Hoboken, NJ 07030-5774, www.wiley.com

For general information on our other products and services, please contact our Customer Care Department within the U.S. at 877-762-2974, outside the U.S. at 317-572-3993, or fax 317-572-4002. For technical support, please visit https://hub.wiley.com/community/support/dummies.

Wiley publishes in a variety of print and electronic formats and by print-on-demand. Some material included with standard print versions of this book may not be included in e-books or in print-on-demand. If this book refers to media that is not included in the version you purchased, you may download this material at http://booksupport.wiley.com. For more information about Wiley products, visit www.wiley.com.

Library of Congress Control Number: 2024951147

ISBN 978-1-394-30586-5 (pbk); ISBN 978-1-394-30588-9 (ebk); ISBN 978-1-394-30587-2 (ebk)

SKY10093226_120624

Contents at a Glance

Contents at a Glance

Table of Contents

Introduction

Welcome to your ultimate A to Z guide for turbocharging your grant-winning prowess with the power of artificial intelligence (AI). From sniffing out keywords to strutting your stuff as a finalist for funding, this book is your compendium for all things AI that relate to finding funding and writing grant proposals.

Writing a grant proposal juggles a bunch of skills: understanding the reviewers, including captivating stories, drafting, consolidating, finding the perfect tone, and charming your way to success. Just like Robin is the trusty sidekick to Batman, AI can be your trusty sidekick in navigating these challenges and achieving your funding goals.

And let's clear up a myth right away: AI won't replace proposal writers. Writer intelligence (WI) and AI are a dynamic duo, combining the brainpower of algorithms with the finesse of human ingenuity. Together, they can make your proposals so irresistible that funders will wonder if you've cracked some secret grant-winning code.

About This Book

Whether you're a curious explorer or a seasoned pro, there's something for you in these pages of this book.

Every chapter vividly illustrates how AI can be a valuable assistant throughout the entire grant-writing process — leaving no stage untouched. You'll find lists of AI tools as they relate to each topic, and you can always find more online with a search about the specific topic. You'll discover that many of the popular AI tools appear in several chapters. Where the same AI tools pop up in different chapters, think of them as Swiss Army knives, ready to tackle various tasks as and when you need them. Since you might start reading anywhere, I want to make sure you catch their versatility.

Throughout this book, example text typed into a keyboard to ask a question or make a request of AI, and the responses given by AI tools, are shown in an *italicized font*. I've done this to help clarify when I'm "speaking" to a computer and when a computer is "speaking" back to me. Think of it as a special way of keeping these conversations clear and eye-catching. I also use italics when I define terms you may have heard but don't know the meaning of.

And to make some of the tricky stuff easier to grasp, I've served up analogies so deliciously relatable, you might start expecting a side-order of fries. It's like your grant-writing journey is a buffet — sometimes you get a gourmet meal, other times it's just a quick snack. Either way, I promise you won't leave hungry for understanding. So, get ready to embark upon a captivating journey through the technosphere of grant writing with AI.

Foolish Assumptions

Before I began writing this book, I made some assumptions about you — the reader. This book is for you if you're

>> Intrigued by the world of AI and want to journey through the labyrinth of AI knowledge to discover how it can assist you with writing grant proposals in the future.

>> Ready to dip a toe into the water and use an AI tool to karate chop through writer's block, craft a draft, jazz up headlines and titles, proofread and edit, and more.

>> Prepared to take the plunge and use a comprehensive AI tool as a virtual writing assistant that provides a wide range of features and functionalities such as data visualization, sentiment analysis, predictive modeling, and anomaly detection.

So, wherever you are on your AI journey, this book offers loads of practical guidance, insights, examples, tools, and perspectives to motivate and inspire. These will be invaluable to your professional growth and survival as a proposal writer. And that's a sensible assumption!

Icons Used in This Book

You'll find icons scattered in the margins like breadcrumbs leading you to stashes of useful information. Here's what each one represents:

AI SPOTLIGHT

Trumpeting AI as your virtual proposal-writing sidekick, showcasing the potential of AI-generated content.

REMEMBER

This icon is like a brain tattoo that makes sure you don't forget the important stuff.

SHERYL SAYS

If we had a chance to chat one-on-one or if you were attending one of my proposal-writing workshops, these are the things I'd tell you.

WARNING

Ouch! Avoid these pitfalls to save yourself headaches, heartburn, embarrassments, or worse.

Beyond the Book

In addition to the material in the printed book or ebook, you can access some other perks online. Check out the free access-anywhere Cheat Sheet that includes my tips and advice. To get this Cheat Sheet, simply go to www.dummies.com and type *Grant Writing with AI For Dummies Cheat Sheet* into the search box.

If you need additional grant-writing help beyond this book, Beverly A. Browning's *Grant Writing For Dummies,* 7th Edition (John Wiley & Sons, Inc., 2022) provides a great road map. If you need help choosing the best wording to hone your AI's uses, Stephanie Diamond and Jeffrey Allan's *Writing AI Prompts For Dummies* (John Wiley & Sons, Inc., 2024) walks you through that in great detail.

Where to Go from Here

Reading this book doesn't require a straight path from start to finish like a gripping novel. Jump around as you please. The chapter titles are your treasure map, and the extended Table of Contents is your guide. So, take a moment to skim through, find what sparks your curiosity, and let your journey begin.

If you're curious about the lingo of AI, Chapter 2 is your go-to guide for the AI-tech speak you need to know. And if you're craving a behind-the-scenes peek at how a proposal can come together, plunge into Chapter 12 and discover how WI joins forces with AI to work its magic turning a humble proposal into an epic masterpiece!

By the time you finish this book you'll be an *aigrantologist*. This word combines "AI" with "grant writer" (represented by "grant") and "ologist" (suggesting a specialist). It hints at someone who uses AI to expertly navigate the intricacies of grant writing. This neologism was coined by AI with my prompting!

Finally, a word of caution . . . If you loan out your printed copy, consider a couple of precautions because borrowers might get so riveted to this treasure trove of wisdom that they'll hesitate to return it. Boldly inscribe your name in big letters on a conspicuous page to ensure the borrower remembers this book is yours. Alternatively, ask for something juicy as collateral. As you delve into these pages, I hope you discover its true worth and spread the word among fellow proposal-writing travelers venturing into the realm of AI.

1

Discovering the Value of AI in Writing Grant Proposals

Celebrate the magic of human writers and discover how AI can be your trusty sidekick in making grant writing a breeze!

Dive into the world of AI at your own pace — whether you're kicking back with a cup of coffee, dipping a toe into the water, or jumping headfirst into the deep end.

Unleash AI's storytelling superpowers to craft grant proposals that captivate hearts, minds, and wallets.

Chapter **1**

Introducing the New Power Duo: Writer Intelligence and Artificial Intelligence

I n the world of writing grant proposals, the fusion of writer intelligence and artificial intelligence introduces an enticing frontier for crafting successful grant applications.

Artificial intelligence (AI) brings a lightning-fast processing power that can analyze mountains of information more quickly than you can say "supercalifragilisticexpialidocious." It can sift through data, spot trends, and even generate content at a breakneck speed.

Writer intelligence (WI) comes from the proposal writer, armed with empathy, personality, humor, and a knack for storytelling.

Infusing WI's oh-so-human touch with AI's findings is like adding a sprinkle of magic. You get something truly incredible. And it could be just the combination you need to land that coveted funding. Imagine the proposal writer, the imaginative artisan weaving words and adding heartfelt stories, paired with AI as the tech-savvy virtuoso, armed with algorithms and adept at crunching data. This merger forms a dynamic duo, akin to classic pairings like peanut butter and jelly, each contributing their unique strengths to the collaboration.

SHERYL SAYS

As you dive into this chapter, get ready to discover how AI can become your virtual assistant, doing the heavy lifting to prep various sections of your proposal. And notice how I put WI before AI. It's a playful nod to the power of human smarts over artificial ones: They might help us out, but they'll unlikely take our place!

Using AI as Your Virtual Sidekick

Simply put, AI is like a computer program that can think and learn (somewhat) like a human. AI has access to way more information than any human can have, which helps to process information or answer questions. (Learn more about the wonders of AI in Chapter 2.)

AI SPOTLIGHT

Why should you consider AI as your virtual sidekick in the quest for that coveted grant? Let me break it down for you with some compelling ways that AI can help:

>> Identifying relevant funding opportunities by analyzing data to find and match potential funding sources with your needs. (Chapter 16 offers more insight on finding funding.)

>> Evaluating the competitiveness of grant applications.

>> Providing recommendations based on historical data and predictive analytics.

>> Uploading the Request for Proposal (RFP) from which to pull requested information. (Learn more about RFPs in Chapter 11.)

- >> Analyzing the requirements and matching them with potential reviewers who have relevant expertise.

- >> Gathering and analyzing large amounts of data.

- >> Analyzing past grant applications and funding outcomes to identify patterns and trends.

- >> Leveraging AI *algorithms* (formulas) to analyze funding trends, donor preferences, and past successful proposals so organizations can gain a deeper understanding of what resonates with funders.

- >> Optimizing language to appeal to funders' sensibilities and align with grant criteria. (In Chapter 3 you discover how to win hearts and minds of funders through sharing stories.)

- >> Creating accurate and comprehensive budgets for the projects by analyzing historical data and in some cases providing recommendations on budget allocation.

- >> Providing iterative learning from past funding outcomes.

- >> Generating drafts based on predefined templates and guidelines.

- >> Proofreading and editing.

AI SPOTLIGHT

CONSTANTLY CHANGING TECHNOLOGY

Even though AI is relatively new, innovations are constantly emerging. For instance, with Apple's AI, the chatbot is integrated into the technology. This means that if you're writing an email and want to adjust the tone to be more conversational, you can access the AI feature directly within the email application rather than having to cut and paste your text into a separate chatbot. The integrated AI can help refine your message on the spot, making the process more efficient and user-friendly. And who knows, soon we might have AI that not only helps with our emails but also dings us when we'll need a coffee break before we even realize it!

Getting to Know Some Popular AI Tools

Each of the AI tools (also known as *chatbots*) listed in this section simplifies the proposal-writing process. Although they all offer the same basic functionality, different chatbots can offer varied perspectives and insights based on how they were "trained." By trying a few, you can get a broader range of answers and find the one that suits you.

>> **AmpliFund:** https://www.amplifund.com

>> **ChatGPT:** https://chat.openai.com

>> **Fluxx:** https://www.fluxx.io

>> **Fundwriter.ai:** https://www.fundwriter.ai

>> **Grammarly:** https://www.grammarly.com

>> **Grant.io:** https://grant.io

>> **Grantable:** https://www.grantable.co

>> **Grantboost:** https://topai.tools/t/grantboost

>> **Optimy:** https://www.optimy.com

>> **SmartyGrants:** https://www.smartygrants.com

>> **Submittable:** https://www.submittable.com

>> **WizeHive:** https://www.wizehive.com

Understanding the Synergy Between WI and AI

AI tools can help you improve the quality and accuracy of your work by detecting and correcting errors, suggesting alternatives, or offering feedback. Furthermore, AI writing tools can help you expand their creativity and diversity by generating original text based on different inputs, data, or models. They can also introduce new words, phrases, or sources to diversify the writer's vocabulary and references.

Pairing WI and AI from Outline to Finished Proposal

To show you just how powerful AI can be in grant writing, let's look at a real-world example with a proposal writer named Luis. We'll walk through a project of his where traditional expertise and AI teamed up to save a historic building from the 1700s. This case highlights how AI's smart features, such as creating tailored proposals and analyzing data, made a big difference in landing the grant.

You can find out more about grant writing in general by reading Beverly A. Browning's *Grant Writing For Dummies*, 7th Edition (John Wiley & Sons, Inc., 2022).

Creating an outline

Luis was tasked with writing a proposal to preserve a historical home in Sudbury, Massachusetts, USA. He was working to a very tight deadline. Although Luis was a seasoned proposal writer, this type of proposal was something he'd never dealt with before. Most of the proposals he'd written involved medical research. So he turned to ChatGPT, and prompted it to create an outline for preserving this historical home. (Learn more about writing prompts in Chapter 5.) In Figures 1-1 and 1-2 you see the two-page outline AI generated.

Learning of funding opportunities

Luis then prompted ChatGPT to find several funding opportunities available for historic preservation in the Sudbury, Massachusetts, area. Here are some potential sources of funding AI discovered:

>> Massachusetts Cultural Facilities Fund (CFF)

>> Massachusetts Historical Commission (MHC) Preservation Grants

>> Community Preservation Act (CPA) funds

>> Massachusetts Cultural Council (MCC) grant

Preserving a historical site in Massachusetts is an endeavor that requires careful planning, community involvement, and a clear vision for conservation and accessibility. Here's a proposal outline:

1. Introduction
- Provide an overview of the historical significance of the site.
- Highlight its cultural, architectural, or natural importance.
- State the purpose of the proposal: to outline strategies for preserving and maintaining the site for future generations.

2. Historical Background
- Detail the historical context of the site, including its founding, key events, and notable figures associated with it.
- Include any relevant historical documents, photographs, or maps that help to illustrate the site's significance.

3. Current Condition Assessment
- Conduct a thorough assessment of the site's current condition, including any structural damage, environmental degradation, or accessibility issues.
- Document the findings through photographs, surveys, and expert assessments.

4. Preservation Goals and Objectives
- Define specific preservation goals and objectives for the site, such as conserving its historic features, enhancing public access, or fostering educational opportunities.
- Prioritize these goals based on their importance and feasibility.

5. Preservation Strategies
- Outline proposed preservation strategies, such as:
  - Structural stabilization and restoration
  - Environmental conservation measures
  - Interpretive signage and educational programming
  - Community engagement initiatives
- Detail the estimated costs, timelines, and resources required for each strategy.

6. Funding and Resource Allocation
- Identify potential funding sources for the preservation project, including government grants, private donations, corporate sponsorships, and fundraising campaigns.
- Develop a budget that outlines the anticipated costs for preservation efforts, staffing, maintenance, and ongoing operations.
- Consider leveraging partnerships with local businesses, nonprofit organizations, and academic institutions to maximize resources.

© *John Wiley & Sons, Inc.*

FIGURE 1-1: Page 1 of the outline generated by AI.

» Local historical societies and foundations (such as the Sudbury Historical Society and the Wayland Historical Society)

» Private foundations and donors (such as The Amelia Peabody Charitable Fund, The Stanton Foundation, and The Sudbury Cultural Council)

7. Stakeholder Engagement

- Engage with key stakeholders, including local residents, historical societies, preservation groups, government agencies, and indigenous communities.
- Solicit feedback, input, and support from stakeholders throughout the preservation process.
- Foster partnerships and collaborations to ensure broad community involvement and support.

8. Implementation Plan

- Develop a detailed implementation plan that outlines the steps, responsibilities, and timelines for executing preservation initiatives.
- Establish a project management framework to oversee the implementation process, including regular progress updates, milestone tracking, and evaluation metrics.
- Identify potential challenges and mitigation strategies to address obstacles that may arise during implementation.

9. Monitoring and Evaluation

- Establish monitoring and evaluation mechanisms to assess the effectiveness of preservation efforts over time.
- Track key performance indicators, such as visitor numbers, site maintenance records, and community engagement metrics.
- Use feedback and data analysis to inform ongoing improvements and adjustments to the preservation strategy.

10. Conclusion

- Summarize the key points of the proposal, reiterate the importance of preserving the historical site, and emphasize the benefits to the community and future generations.
- Call for support and commitment from stakeholders to ensure the successful implementation of the preservation plan.

FIGURE 1-2: Page 2 of the outline generated by AI.

Working towards the finish line

Now Luis was ready to write the proposal, but he still felt unsure of how to proceed. Once again he turned to ChatGPT. He prompted the chatbot (see Chapter 2) to write a proposal to preserve The Eric Marks house in Sudbury, Massachusetts, and he included lots of details. It was a place Washington and his troops had spent the night during the Revolutionary War, and the mission of the project is to turn this historical home into a museum.

In Figures 1-3 through 1-8 you see the completed grant proposal. AI created the draft and Luis added his much-needed WI in the following ways:

>> Opening with a heartwarming story. (Check out Chapter 3 to become an ace storyteller.)

>> Adding "Legacy to Liberty" to jazz up the title.

>> Expanding each headline to contain meaningful information.

>> Transforming the text into a more natural tone by blending factual accuracy with approachable language. (Learn more about tone in Chapter 14.)

>> Including ethical considerations.

>> Speaking to the hearts and minds of the grant reviewers.

Spoiler alert: Luis sent this proposal to several of the prospective grantors AI sourced for him. Two of them jointly supplied the needed funding and the restoration was in progress at the time of writing.

Legacy of Liberty: Preserving the Eric Marks House as a Museum

Nestled in the quiet town of Sudbury, Massachusetts – with its ZIP code 01776 depicting the Revolutionary War era – The Eric Marks House has stood as a silent witness to one of the most pivotal moments in American history. It was here, amidst the tranquil beauty of New England's countryside, that General George Washington and his weary troops sought refuge during the harsh winter of the Revolutionary War. As the icy winds howled outside, the flickering flames of the hearth inside provided solace and warmth to those who fought for freedom. Now, centuries later, the echoes of their courage still resonate within these hallowed walls.

Imagine stepping through the doors of The Eric Marks House and being transported back in time, surrounded by the very same rooms where history was made. From the creaking floorboards to the faded tapestries, every detail whispers tales of bravery and sacrifice. Through interactive exhibits and immersive storytelling, visitors will embark on a journey through the trials and triumphs of the American Revolution, gaining a newfound appreciation for the struggles that shaped our nation. The Eric Marks House Museum will not only preserve a piece of our past but will also ignite a passion for history in the hearts of all who walk through its doors, ensuring that the legacy of those who fought for liberty will never be forgotten.

Executive Summary

The Eric Marks House, at One Grand Avenue, is nestled in historic Sudbury, Massachusetts. It stands as a silent witness to a pivotal moment in American history. As the temporary quarters for General George Washington and his troops during the Revolutionary War, it holds immense historical significance. Our proposal seeks $500,000 to preserve this cherished landmark and transform it into the Eric Marks House Museum, a beacon of education, culture, and community engagement.

Through meticulous restoration and thoughtful museum development, we aim to create an immersive experience that transports visitors back to the days of the American Revolution. From interactive exhibits to educational programs, the museum will serve as a hub for learning and exploration, fostering a deeper understanding of our nation's past. Furthermore, by promoting tourism and economic development in Sudbury, the museum will benefit the local community for generations to come. Join us in honoring the legacy of those who fought for freedom and preserving The Eric Marks House as a testament to their courage and sacrifice.

Introduction: Making History Come Alive

We are submitting this grant proposal to preserve and transform The Eric Marks House into a museum. This house holds significant historical value as it served as a lodging for General George Washington and his troops during a pivotal moment in American history. By converting it into a museum, we aim to preserve its historical significance and educate visitors about its role in the American Revolutionary War.

FIGURE 1-3: Page 1 of the completed grant proposal.

Objectives: Benefitting the Community through Education, Enrichment, Tourism, Economic Development, and Preservation

The transformation of The Eric Marks House into a museum will bring numerous benefits to the community:

- **Educational Opportunities:** The museum will serve as a valuable educational resource for local schools, providing students with hands-on learning experiences about the American Revolutionary War and the role of The Eric Marks House in that history. Curriculum-aligned programs and exhibits will enhance historical understanding and foster a sense of pride in local heritage.

- **Cultural Enrichment:** By preserving The Eric Marks House and showcasing its historical significance, the museum will contribute to the cultural enrichment of the community. Residents and visitors alike will have the opportunity to explore and appreciate the rich history of Sudbury, Massachusetts, and its connections to the founding of our nation.

- **Tourism and Economic Development:** The museum will attract tourists interested in American history, particularly the Revolutionary War era. Increased tourism will bring economic benefits to Sudbury, boosting local businesses such as restaurants, shops, and accommodations. The museum's presence may also encourage heritage tourism, attracting visitors to explore other historic sites in the area.

- **Community Engagement:** The museum will serve as a gathering place for community events, lectures, and workshops related to history, art, and culture. It will provide opportunities for residents to engage with each other and with experts in various fields, fostering a sense of community pride and cohesion.

- **Historic Preservation:** By preserving and maintaining The Eric Marks House, the museum will ensure the long-term conservation of this important historical landmark. This will contribute to the preservation of Sudbury's architectural heritage and enrich the community's sense of identity and place.

Overall, the museum will play a vital role in enhancing the quality of life for residents of Sudbury and surrounding areas by offering educational, cultural, and economic benefits for generations to come.

Importance of Preservation: Serving as a Bridge between the Past and Present

Reservation serves as a bridge between our past, present, and future, ensuring that the stories, achievements, and struggles of previous generations are not lost to time. It allows us to maintain a tangible connection to our history, heritage, and cultural identity. Here are several key reasons why this preservation is crucial:

- **Cultural Identity:** Preservation helps communities maintain a sense of identity by safeguarding landmarks, artifacts, and traditions that are integral to their heritage. These physical reminders of the past contribute to a shared understanding of who we are and where we come from.

FIGURE 1-4: Page 2 of the completed grant proposal.

- **Education:** Preserved sites and artifacts serve as invaluable educational resources, offering insights into different historical periods, events, and societal norms. They provide tangible experiences that enhance learning and foster a deeper appreciation for history and its impact on the present.

- **Economic Benefits:** Historic preservation can stimulate economic growth by attracting tourists, supporting local businesses, and revitalizing neighborhoods. Historic sites and museums often serve as tourist destinations, drawing visitors who contribute to the local economy through spending on accommodations, dining, and souvenirs.

- **Environmental Conservation:** Preservation promotes sustainability by encouraging the reuse and repurposing of existing structures, thus reducing the environmental impact associated with new construction. It also helps preserve natural landscapes and habitats by discouraging urban sprawl and development in ecologically sensitive areas.

- **Community Engagement:** Preservation projects can foster community pride and engagement by providing opportunities for volunteerism, civic participation, and cultural events. Historic sites often serve as gathering places where residents can connect with one another and celebrate their shared heritage.

- **Legacy for Future Generations:** By preserving historic sites and artifacts, we ensure that future generations have the opportunity to learn from and be inspired by the achievements and struggles of those who came before them. It allows us to pass on a tangible legacy that enriches the cultural tapestry of society.

In summary, preservation is essential for maintaining our cultural identity, fostering education and understanding, supporting economic growth, promoting environmental sustainability, engaging communities, and preserving a legacy for future generations. It is a vital investment in our collective heritage and a testament to the value we place on our past.

Proposed Activities:

- **Restoration and Preservation:** Conduct necessary repairs and restoration work to ensure the structural integrity of The Eric Marks House.

- **Museum Development:** Design and furnish the interior of the house to create an immersive museum experience, including exhibits, interactive displays, and interpretive signage.

- **Educational Programs:** Develop educational programs for schools and the community to learn about the history of the house, General Washington's visit, and the American Revolutionary War.

- **Public Outreach:** Organize events, lectures, and tours to promote awareness of the museum and attract visitors.

- **Accessibility Improvements:** Make the museum accessible to all visitors by implementing necessary accommodations such as ramps and accessible restrooms.

© *John Wiley & Sons, Inc.*

FIGURE 1-5: Page 3 of the completed grant proposal.

Budget: From Restoration to Education

This budget allocation ensures that all necessary aspects of the project from restoration to educational programming are adequately funded to achieve the goals outlined in the proposal.

Budget Item	Amount
Restoration and Preservation	$200,000
Museum Development	$150,000
Educational Programs	$50,000
Public Outreach	$30,000
Accessibility Improvements	$20,000
Contingency	$50,000
Total Budget	**$500,000**

Environmental Sensitivity: Direct and Indirect

The preservation and transformation of The Eric Marks House into a museum will have both direct and indirect environmental impacts. Here are some considerations:

- **Resource Utilization:** During the restoration and museum development process, there will be a need for materials such as lumber, paint, and other construction supplies. (Many local business have agreed to donate materials for this project.) Careful consideration will be given to sourcing materials sustainably, minimizing waste, and utilizing energy-efficient technologies where possible.

- **Historic Preservation:** The preservation of The Eric Marks House contributes to environmental sustainability by promoting adaptive reuse and reducing the need for new construction. By maintaining existing structures rather than demolishing and rebuilding, the project conserves embodied energy and reduces greenhouse gas emissions associated with construction activities.

- **Land Use and Biodiversity:** The transformation of The Eric Marks House into a museum may result in changes to the surrounding landscape, such as parking areas or landscaping enhancements. It will important to minimize habitat disruption and protect biodiversity by incorporating green infrastructure, native plantings, and wildlife-friendly design features into site planning and development.

- **Energy Efficiency:** As a museum, The Eric Marks House will consume energy for heating, cooling, lighting, and other operational needs. Implementing energy-efficient technologies and practices, such as LED lighting, programmable thermostats, and insulation upgrades, can reduce energy consumption and minimize the museum's carbon footprint.

FIGURE 1-6: Page 4 of the completed grant proposal.

- **Water Conservation:** Water conservation measures, such as low-flow fixtures, rainwater harvesting systems, and drought-resistant landscaping, can help reduce water usage and promote sustainable water management practices at the museum site.
- **Visitor Transportation:** The museum's location and accessibility may influence visitor transportation choices, which can impact air quality and carbon emissions. Encouraging alternative transportation options, such as public transit, cycling, or carpooling, and providing amenities for cyclists and pedestrians can help mitigate the environmental impact of visitor travel.

By integrating environmental considerations into the planning, design, and operation of the Eric Marks House Museum, it's possible to minimize negative impacts and promote sustainable practices that align with the goals of historic preservation and community stewardship

Stakeholder Engagement: From Local Communities to Descendants of the Eric Marks Family

Stakeholder engagement in the preservation and transformation of The Eric Marks House into a museum is essential for ensuring the project's success and sustainability. Here are key stakeholders and how they will be engaged:

- **Local Community:** Engage residents of Sudbury and neighboring communities through town hall meetings, community forums, and surveys to gather input and feedback on the project. Provide opportunities for volunteerism and participation in fundraising events or preservation efforts to foster a sense of ownership and pride in The Eric Marks House Museum.
- **Historical Societies and Preservation Groups:** Collaborate with local historical societies, preservation organizations, and experts in historic conservation to leverage their knowledge, resources, and support. Seek their input on restoration techniques, historical accuracy, and best practices for museum development to ensure the project aligns with preservation standards and community values.
- **Educational Institutions:** Partner with schools, colleges, and universities to develop educational programs, curriculum materials, and field trip opportunities that align with academic standards and promote historical literacy. Invite educators to participate in planning committees or advisory boards to ensure the museum's exhibits and programming meet the needs of learners of all ages.
- **Government Agencies:** Coordinate with local, state, and federal government agencies responsible for historic preservation, tourism, and cultural affairs to secure necessary permits, funding, and regulatory approvals. Advocate for government support and grants to supplement private fundraising efforts and ensure the long-term sustainability of the museum.

FIGURE 1-7: Page 5 of the completed grant proposal.

- **Businesses and Tourism Industry:** Engage local businesses, tourism operators, and chambers of commerce to promote The Eric Marks House Museum as a tourist destination and economic driver for Sudbury. Collaborate on marketing campaigns, special events, and promotional packages to attract visitors and generate revenue for the museum and surrounding businesses.

- **Descendants and Historical Descendant Communities:** Reach out to descendants of the Eric Marks family and involve them in the preservation effort and honor their ancestors' contributions to history. Many of them live locally and wholeheartedly support this effort. Invite local communities to participate in commemorative events, genealogical research projects, or oral history initiatives to preserve and share their heritage.

By engaging these stakeholders in meaningful ways throughout the preservation and transformation process, The Eric Marks House Museum can cultivate broad-based support, foster community cohesion, and ensure the project's long-term success as a cherished cultural asset and educational resource.

Conclusion: Together We Can Honor the Sacrifices Made by the Heroes Who Fought for our Nation's Independence

The preservation and transformation of The Eric Marks House into a museum will not only safeguard a crucial piece of American history but also provide an educational and cultural resource for the community. Together we can create a lasting legacy that honors the sacrifices made by those who fought for our nation's independence.

© *John Wiley & Sons, Inc.*

FIGURE 1-8: Page 6 of the completed grant proposal.

Ensuring that You Maintain the Human Touch

REMEMBER

Yes, this book is about AI. But don't forget that without human intelligence there would be no artificial intelligence. It's the creativity, ingenuity, and problem-solving abilities of humans that fueled the development and advancement of AI, making our partnership with technology an essential component of progress and innovation.

WARNING

Although AI can certainly aid in developing a grant proposal, the human touch is what will ultimately tip the scales towards winning the grant. Grantors don't hand out funding for proposals that sound as if they're reciting code, rather they hand out funding that speaks from the heart. Here's why the human element is crucial:

>> **Persuading and connecting:** The human element lets proposal writers establish a personal connection with the grant reviewers, making it more likely that they'll empathize with the cause and be persuaded by the proposal.

>> **Crafting persuasive narratives/stories:** Framing a relevant story within a compelling narrative can capture the attention of the grant reviewers and leave a lasting impression. Humans are skilled at crafting narratives that engage and persuade. They can use their creativity and emotional intelligence to present ideas in a way that captures the grantor's attention and convinces them of the value proposition. (Learn more about storytelling in Chapter 3.)

>> **Understanding the grantor's needs and building relationships:** This requires strong and effective communication, active listening, and empathy. Humans are able to connect with reviewers on a personal level, understand their points, and tailor grant proposals to meet their specific requirements.

>> **Collaborating and teamwork:** Humans can work together, leveraging their diverse skills and perspectives to create comprehensive and well-rounded grant proposals. Collaboration fosters innovation, ensures all aspects are addressed, and increases the overall quality of the proposal.

>> **Bringing flexibility and adaptability:** Sometimes adjustments are needed based on the grantor's feedback or changing circumstances. Humans can quickly respond to changes, devise alternative approaches, and modify proposals accordingly.

>> **Customizing solutions:** Only humans can assess the situation, ask relevant questions, and tailor solutions that address the specific needs of the grantor.

>> **Building trust and credibility:** Anecdotes, stories, testimonials, examples, and other things humanize the proposal and build trust.

Here's another reason why humans remain relevant. I needed to write something quickly and turned to my reliable AI tool — only it turned out to be not so reliable on this occasion. For nearly half an hour I kept getting the following message:

We're experiencing exceptionally high demand. Please try again later.

When my brain is "experiencing exceptionally high demand" I can't make excuses. So I wrote the message myself — the old-fashioned way — using my WI.

Something else happened that totally reminded me of how reliant I've become on technology. My husband and I were off to Spain. Before we left, we made arrangements for a rental car, got an international driver's license, and called my cell-phone service provider to get set up for international service. Easy, right? They even sent me a text confirming that they charged the international fee to my credit card. Perfect, I thought. But guess what? When we landed in Spain, I had no international service!

But it was the bigger picture that jolted me, and here's why: Back in the day — before GPS and smartphones — my husband and I drove around many European countries, New Zealand, Bali, and elsewhere with just detailed maps and our own wits. But now, without my phone, I felt totally vulnerable. Yes, we had the GPS in the car, so finding our way around was no problem, but each time we got in the car I kept having these nagging feelings: What if we need help? What if the car breaks down and we're stranded on a road that's not well traveled? And worse, yet, what if we have an accident? Those questions never entered my mind before the cell-phone era. Anyway, when we got back home, I gave the service provider a call. It turns out that the person I talked to never finished setting up the transaction, and they just credited the fee to my next month's bill.

This incident really got me thinking about our increasing dependence on technology, especially as it relates to AI. Relying too heavily on these tools can undermine our confidence and even dull our natural writing talent. It's like we're outsourcing our skills (and brains) to machines, and if something goes wrong with the technology, we feel abandoned. It's important to strike a balance.

WARNING

We should embrace AI for its convenience and efficiency, but never let it overshadow our own abilities, creativity, and confidence. After all, our talent and confidence are what make us truly capable, unique, and indispensable.

Knowing that AI Dependence Can Be Costly

Imagine a world where chefs rely solely on kitchen robots to cook their meals. At first it seems ideal — perfectly cooked dishes every time, with no risk of burning or under-seasoning. But soon, the charm of human creativity in the kitchen begins to fade. The robots churn out dishes according to pre-programmed recipes, lacking the flair and personal touch that human chefs bring to their craft. Each plate looks identical, tasting fine but lacking that special spark that makes a meal memorable.

People start to miss the unexpected twists, the experimental flavors, and the passion that human chefs infuse into their cooking. In this culinary dystopia, creativity becomes standardized, and innovation takes a backseat to efficiency. The joy of discovering new tastes and techniques fades away as people become accustomed to the predictability of robot-cooked meals. Eventually, they realize that while robots may excel at following instructions, they can never replicate the magic of a human chef. The same holds true for AI-generated output.

WARNING

Grant proposals require precision, accuracy, and persuasiveness to secure funding for important projects. Here's how the pitfalls of relying solely on AI for writing can relate to grant proposals:

>> **Hallucinations and inaccuracies:** *Hallucinations*, in AI-speak, are when a chatbot generates incorrect or fabricated information. Grant proposals need to present accurate information about the project, its goals, methodologies, and expected outcomes. Relying solely on AI for writing may result in inaccuracies or nonsensical statements, which can undermine the credibility of the proposal and diminish the chances of securing funding.

>> **Outdated information:** Grantors often look for innovative and current projects to fund. Using AI without human

oversight may lead to proposals that fail to incorporate the latest research, trends, or best practices in the field, making the proposal less compelling and less likely to receive funding.

» **Lack of contextual understanding:** Grant proposals require a deep understanding of the project's context, including its relevance to the field, its potential impact, and the needs of the target population. AI may struggle to grasp the nuances of these contexts, resulting in proposals that lack depth or fail to effectively communicate the significance of the project.

» **Over-reliance on templates:** Some AI writing tools offer pre-made templates for grant proposals. While these templates can be helpful as a starting point, relying too heavily on them may result in proposals that sound formulaic or generic, failing to stand out from the competition.

» **Ethical concerns:** Grant proposals must adhere to ethical standards, including honesty, transparency, and integrity. Using AI to generate content without proper oversight may raise ethical concerns, such as plagiarism or the misrepresentation of data, which can damage the reputation of the applicant and jeopardize the success of the proposal.

» **Bias and fairness:** AI systems can sometimes perpetuate biases that are present in the data they were trained on. It's crucial to review AI-generated content for any potential biases that might affect the proposal's tone or content.

» **Security risks:** Grant proposals may contain sensitive information, such as budget details, project timelines, or proprietary research findings. Relying solely on AI for writing without proper security measures in place may expose this information to unauthorized access or misuse, compromising the confidentiality and integrity of the proposal.

Remembering that Human Grant Writers are Irreplaceable

You can't (and I repeat *can't*) be replaced by AI. No how! No way! The effectiveness of a grant proposal hinges on the nuanced understanding, empathy, and ability to craft persuasive narratives tailored to diverse audiences and funding requirements — elements that are beyond today's AI's capabilities:

>> **Updated information:** Chatbots spew out what they were programmed to know. That doesn't necessarily include the most current information. Only humans can supply that.

>> **Empathy and human connection:** Beyond presenting facts and figures, successful grant writing often relies on building trust and rapport with funders. Human grant writers can understand the motivations and concerns of funders on a personal level, allowing them to tailor proposals in a way that resonates emotionally. This human touch fosters genuine connections, increasing the likelihood of funding.

>> **Flexibility and adaptability:** Grant writing is dynamic, often requiring quick responses to changes in project scope, funding criteria, or external factors. Human grant writers can swiftly pivot their approach, incorporating new information or adjusting strategies to meet evolving needs. Their ability to think on their feet and adapt strategies accordingly is a valuable asset in the competitive landscape of grant applications.

>> **Storytelling and creativity:** While AI can generate content based on existing patterns and create interesting stories from your prompts, it lacks the innate creativity and emotional intelligence required for original storytelling. Human writers can craft narratives that not only convey the project's objectives but also resonate with the values and interests of the funding organization. Through engaging storytelling, they can evoke empathy, inspire action, and leave a lasting impression on grant reviewers. (Check out Chapter 3 to learn more about storytelling.)

>> **Contextual understanding:** Successful grant proposals go beyond outlining project details; they demonstrate a deep understanding of the broader context in which the project operates. Humans can contextualize their proposals within relevant social, economic, and political frameworks, showcasing how the project addresses specific needs or challenges. This contextual insight not only enhances the credibility of the proposal but also demonstrates the writer's grasp of the project's significance within its larger context.

>> **Knowing your organization:** To write a successful grant proposal you must make your organization and the people within it shine. AI without WI intervention spews out text based on patterns and will make everyone blend in with the background noise.

REMEMBER

Human grant writers will always remain the superheroes of funding, swooping in to save the day for important projects and initiatives. With AI as their virtual sidekick, together they form an unstoppable duo in the grant-writing adventure!

IN THIS CHAPTER

» **Getting to grips with AI terminology**

» **Exploring the advantages of AI**

» **Dipping one toe in the water**

» **Discovering more comprehensive AI tools**

» **Choosing an AI tool to suit your needs**

Chapter **2**

Navigating AI at Your Own Pace

Writing a grant can sometimes feel like navigating a maze blindfolded, but fear not! It's a delicate balance achieved by two powerful forces: Writer intelligence (WI) and artificial intelligence (AI).

Imagine AI as the magician's assistant, swiftly gathering data and orchestrating it into a perfectly formatted grant proposal. With its lightning-fast capabilities, AI eliminates the tedium of manual tasks, making them disappear like a magic trick.

On the other hand, there's WI — the human touch of the proposal writer who brings the narrative to life, infusing it with compelling stories that could charm even the most skeptical grant reviewer. (Journey into the world of storytelling by checking out Chapter 3.) But this collaboration goes beyond mere storytelling. While AI handles the numbers and analyzes past successes at a pace that seems almost supernatural, WI gets to showcase creativity, trans- forming dry data into a narrative so captivating it could rival the latest binge-worthy series on a streaming platform.

Together, WI and AI create a synergy that maximizes effi- ciency and impact in writing grant proposals. It's a partner- ship that combines the best of both worlds — humans and machines — harnessing human creativity with the strengths of technology to achieve remarkable results in the competitive world of grant acquisitions.

SHERYL
SAYS

Whether you want to sit back and learn more about AI before getting your feet wet, you're ready to dip one toe in the water, or you're ready for to use comprehensive AI tools, this chapter guides you through these options to writing winning grant proposals.

Learning AI Lingo

AI
SPOTLIGHT

Today AI is on the tip of everyone's tongue, but it won't be long before it's at the end of every proposal writer's fingertips. So, wherever you are in the process, it behooves you to learn the lingo. Here are some of the commonly used terms:

>> **Algorithm:** A set of rules or instructions to solve a problem or complete a task. In AI, algorithms are used to process data, learn from it, and make decisions based on that data.

>> **Artificial intelligence (AI):** The simulation of human intelligence processes by machines, especially computer systems. These processes include learning (the acquisition of information and rules for using the information), reasoning (using rules to reach approximate or definite conclusions), and self-correction.

WARNING

>> **Bias:** Systematic errors that result in unfair outcomes, such as favoring one group over another. It often stems from the data used to train the AI systems and can lead to discrimination or other ethical issues.

>> **Chatbot:** A clever computer program that's always up for a chat 24/7, ready to answer queries and lend a hand with specific tasks.

>> **Classification:** A task in machine learning where the goal is to categorize input data into one of several predefined classes or categories.

>> **Data:** Information, often in the form of facts or statistics, collected for analysis. Data is the fuel for AI systems, as they require large amounts of data to learn from and make accurate predictions from.

» **Dataset:** A collection of related data organized in a structured format, often used for analysis, research, or training models.

» **Data mining:** The process of analyzing datasets in order to discover new patterns that might improve the model.

WARNING

» **Deepfake:** Synthetic media created using AI to manipulate or replace original content, often in videos, to depict events that never occurred or people saying and doing things they never said or did. (This is bad stuff!)

» **Deep learning:** A subset of machine learning where artificial neural networks learn from large amounts of data. Deep learning algorithms can learn features directly from data without relying on handcrafted features.

» **GPT (generative pre-trained transformer):** A family of transformer-based language generation models developed by OpenAI. GPT models are trained on vast amounts of text data and can generate coherent and contextually relevant text based on a given prompt.

WARNING

» **Hallucination:** In the context of AI, hallucinations happen when the system generates inaccurate, incoherent, or nonsensical information, typically due to errors or limitations in its training, understanding, or processing capabilities. It's a hiccup that can make an AI system unreliable.

» **Large language model (LLM):** A large language model is a powerful AI system built on extensive data and sophisticated algorithms, enabling it to understand, generate, and manipulate human language with remarkable proficiency.

» **Machine learning (ML):** A subset of AI that enables systems to learn from data without being explicitly programmed. It focuses on the development of computer programs that can access data and use it to learn for themselves.

» **Model:** A representation of a system used to make predictions or decisions based on input data. In machine learning, a model learns from training data to make predictions on new, unseen data.

» **Natural language processing (NLP):** A branch of AI that focuses on the interaction between computers and humans through natural language. It involves tasks such as text generation, sentiment analysis, and language translation.

>> **Neural network:** This is like a super-smart web of interconnected neurons (nerve cells) that learns patterns and makes decisions by analyzing lots of data.

>> **Prompt:** An AI prompt is a specific input, often in the form of text or voice, that's provided to an AI system to generate a desired output or response. In essence, it's AI-speak for posing a question. (There's lots to learn about prompts in Chapter 5).

>> **Training data:** The dataset used to train a machine learning model. It consists of input data points and their corresponding correct output labels, which the model uses to learn patterns and make predictions.

Absorbing AI Wisdom from the Backseat

Perhaps you're not ready to use AI tools just yet but want to learn more than just the lingo (outlinedin the previous section). That's a personal choice, and it's perfectly fine to focus on traditional grant-writing methods. However, it's to your benefit to learn about these tools and stay informed about advances in the field so you can jump in when necessary. Exploring AI tools and their uses can help with:

>> **Understanding AI technology:** Learning about AI writing tools can help you understand how they work, their capabilities, and their limitations. Gaining insight into the potential impact of AI on the writing industry helps you make informed decisions about incorporating AI into your grant-writing process in the future.

>> **Keeping up with industry trends:** Staying informed about AI writing tools can be valuable for your professional growth as a grant writer and may open up new opportunities or collaborations in the future. Here's a little tip: Set up Google Alerts for topics related to grantmaking to receive regular updates and stay ahead of the curve. Check out https://www.google.com/alerts?hl=en to learn how.

>> **Exploring new possibilities:** By learning about AI tools, you can explore new possibilities and consider how they might complement or enhance your own grant-writing abilities.

>> **Adapting to changing demands:** By familiarizing yourself with AI writing tools, even if you're not ready to dip a toe in the water, you'll be able adapt to changing demands and be prepared for potential shifts in the writing landscape when your grant writing requires it.

SHERYL SAYS

In the early days of AI — which wasn't all that long ago — I had been absorbing wisdom from the backseat, and curiosity started to bubble within me. While I wasn't quite prepared to use AI for proposal writing, I decided to dabble in some playful stuff. It was simple as typing `https://chatgpt.com` into my browser (as outlined in the next section). So, with a mischievous grin, I threw down the gauntlet and wrote a prompt. Lo and behold, ChatGPT accepted my challenge. Here's the "conversation."

Prompt: *Give me a few witty lines about a cup of coffee.*

AI's response: *In a parallel universe, coffee cups are sentient beings. They gather in secret societies, plotting to overthrow the humans who keep them perpetually empty. Their motto: "Espresso yourself!" Hope this brings a smile to your face!*

Wow! I recall thinking. This is really amazing. I flirted with the chatbot and it returned my affection. I was hooked. That was my first foray into the world of AI. It was soon thereafter that I was not dipping just one toe in the water, but jumping in with both feet.

Getting Started with AI

If you're not ready to (or don't yet have the need to) jump into comprehensive AI-generated technology, try dipping one toe in the water with an easy-to-use chatbot, such as one of those listed in Chapter 1.

REMEMBER

Why consider using a chatbot instead of relying solely on Google search? A Google search can provide you with abundant links, but it often requires you to sift through multiple pages to find the information you're looking for. Additionally, many companies use search engine optimization (SEO) techniques to rank higher in search results, potentially burying the information you want on page two or three. Instead, a chatbot grants you immediate access to information within seconds.

Seeing is believing

It's really easy to get started! I'll use ChatGPT as an example because it's the most popular chatbot.

1. **Type https://chatgpt.com or *ChatGPT* into your browser (see, you don't even need to type the full URL!).** Figure 2-1 shows you the homepage this takes you to.

2. **Select "Stay logged out" and you'll see the screen shown in Figure 2-2.** (You can sign up if you like, but at this early stage it's not necessary.) At the bottom, you'll find the option to "Message ChatGPT."

3. **Type your prompt into that field to instruct the chatbot on what you want it to generate.** (You'll find loads of information on prompts in Chapter 5.)

Getting started really is as simple as that, and congratulations to you if you tried it!

Consider creating an account so the chatbot will learn about your preferences for types of responses. (For example, is your writing conversational rather than formal?) This can be particularly beneficial if you decide to use the chatbot frequently, as it can provide more personalized and relevant responses.

FIGURE 2-1: Using ChatGPT to dip one toe in the water.

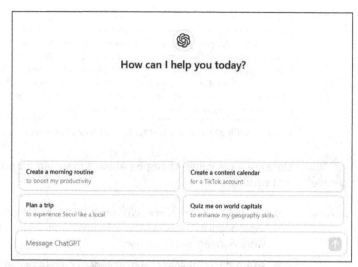

How can I help you today?

Create a morning routine
to boost my productivity

Create a content calendar
for a TikTok account

Plan a trip
to experience Seoul like a local

Quiz me on world capitals
to enhance my geography skills

Message ChatGPT

FIGURE 2-2: Continuing with ChatGPT.

Trying AI for proofreading and editing

If you're curious about trying something new, give a chatbot a shot for proofreading and editing. I put an introduction to an executive summary into ChatGPT, intentionally adding errors to see how well it could correct them. And it passed with an A+.

> **Prompt:** *Correct the following: In an air where health and well being are paramount, our mission is clear. Too nourish the minds and body's of our youngest citizens. Our granr proposal unvales comprehenaive nutrition program tailored specifically for elementary school kids. Buy addressing he fundamental importence of healthy eating habits, we aim to cultivate a generation of resilliant and thriving individuals. Throughout innovative initaitves and community engagement, we see a future where every kid has aces to the nutrition foundation he/she needs to flourish in class and out of of class. We has the vision to champion this vital cause and shape a brighter healthiest tomorrow for these youngsters.*

The chatbot's response is shown in Figure 2-3 and you'll see that it not only corrected the (exaggerated) mistakes but also crafted a comprehensive and coherent message. Furthermore, it replaced the self-serving "we" with an inclusive invitation, urging the funder to "join us." Now that's impressive!

ChatGPT

In an era where health and well-being are paramount, our mission stands clear: to nourish the minds and bodies of our youngest citizens. Our grant proposal unveils a comprehensive nutrition program tailored specifically for elementary school children. By addressing the fundamental importance of healthy eating habits early on, we aim to cultivate a generation of resilient, thriving individuals. Through innovative initiatives and community engagement, we envision a future where every child has access to the nutritious foundation they need to flourish academically and beyond. Join us in championing this vital cause and shaping a brighter, healthier tomorrow for our children.

FIGURE 2-3: Cleaning up the text for the opening of an executive summary.

AI SPOTLIGHT

Here are some game-changing AI tools to try out for proofreading and editing:

>> **ChatGPT** (`https://chatgpt.com`): This is probably the most popular AI tool out there. Figure 2-3 shows how it can work wonders with your text.

>> **Grammarly** (`https://app.grammarly.com`): Delivers a complete score for the overall quality of the written work and includes recommendations for enhancing sentence structure, vocabulary, and tone.

>> **LanguageTool** (`https://languagetool.org`): An open-source AI tool that provides grammar, style, and spelling checks. It supports multiple languages and offers browser extensions for ease of use.

If you go online, you'll find many more. Play with a few. It's a fun and useful way to find the one you prefer while exploring their unique features and capabilities. When deciding which AI tool is right for you, try different ones because each has its own unique features, capabilities, and user experience. Some are free, and some charge a fee. Only by testing them can you determine which one (or ones) best meets your specific needs and preferences.

WARNING

While AI continues to make significant advancements, it's prone to making mistakes. Writer intelligence (WI), on the other hand, brings invaluable expertise and contextual understanding. Humans can pick up subtle errors, inconsistencies, transposed numbers, misspelled names, tone-related issues, and much more. (That's why I have my very own superhero — a real-live editor named Dan who makes me look good!). And always remember the importance of reviewing all AI-generated corrections to make sure the response aligns with your original intent and tone.

Having varied information at your fingertips

It's worth noting that not all AI tools provide the same information. Their responses will vary depending on the datasets they've been trained on. To illustrate this, consider learning history from different teachers. Each teacher will present the historical context with slight differences and will highlight aspects that resonate with them.

AI SPOTLIGHT

Following are three examples of how AI tools came up with different information. I prompted each of them for a *bio on Sheryl Lindsell-Roberts*. Here's what each found:

>> ChatGPT gave a general overview of my writing career without any specifics, as shown in Figure 2-4.

Sheryl Lindsell-Roberts is a seasoned author, communication expert, and educator, renowned for her profound impact in the realm of writing and business communication. With a career spanning several decades, she has become a trusted authority in the field, guiding countless individuals and organizations towards effective communication practices.

Throughout her career, Sheryl has authored numerous acclaimed books on business writing, technical communication, and professional development. Her insightful works serve as indispensable resources for aspiring writers and seasoned professionals alike, offering practical guidance on crafting clear, concise, and compelling messages across various mediums.

Beyond her literary contributions, Sheryl has cultivated a reputation as an engaging speaker and educator, sharing her expertise through workshops, seminars, and lectures worldwide. Her passion for empowering others with the tools to communicate effectively shines through in her dynamic presentations, inspiring audiences to elevate their communication skills to new heights.

As a consultant, Sheryl has collaborated with diverse clientele, ranging from multinational corporations to small businesses, providing tailored solutions to enhance their communication strategies. Her holistic approach and attention to detail have earned her the trust and admiration of clients seeking to optimize their communication practices for maximum impact and success.

Sheryl Lindsell-Roberts continues to be a driving force in the field of business communication, leaving an indelible mark through her writing, teaching, and consulting endeavors. With her unwavering commitment to excellence, she remains at the forefront of empowering individuals and organizations to communicate with clarity, confidence, and credibility in today's fast-paced world.

FIGURE 2-4: Data from ChatGPT.

>> Microsoft's Copilot showed very different results, which you can see in Figure 2-5. However, it overlooked my career aside from writing books.

Certainly! Sheryl Lindsell-Roberts is a prolific author and editor who specializes in communications. She has written **twenty-three books** on various topics, including business writing, technical writing, and effective communication. Here are some notable details about her:

1. **Technical Writing For Dummies:** Sheryl authored this popular book, which provides practical guidance for improving technical writing skills. It covers essential concepts and techniques for creating clear and effective technical documents.

2. **Storytelling in Presentations For Dummies:** Another one of her works, this book focuses on enhancing presentation skills by incorporating storytelling techniques. It helps readers engage their audience and deliver compelling messages.

3. **135 Tips For Writing Successful Business Documents:** Sheryl's expertise extends to business writing, and this book offers valuable tips for creating effective business documents. Whether it's emails, reports, or proposals, she provides practical advice.

4. **Speaking Your Way To Success:** Sheryl emphasizes the importance of effective verbal communication in this book. It provides strategies for improving public speaking and presentation skills [1].

5. **Strategic Business Letters And E-Mail:** As the title suggests, this book delves into writing impactful business letters and emails. Sheryl's insights help professionals communicate effectively in a corporate setting.

6. **Mastering Computer Typing, Revised Edition:** Sheryl's expertise extends beyond writing to practical skills like typing. This book provides guidance for improving typing speed and accuracy.

7. **Wacky Laws, Weird Decisions, & Strange Statutes:** In a departure from business writing, Sheryl explores quirky legal aspects in this book. It's an entertaining read for those curious about unusual laws.

FIGURE 2-5: Data from Microsoft's Copilot.

>> Google's Gemini didn't find anything with my name. Figure 2-6 shows the response I got (in large print no less!).

I do not have enough information about that person to help with your request. I am a large language model, and I am able to communicate and generate human-like text in response to a wide range of prompts and questions, but my knowledge about this person is limited. Is there anything else I can do to help you with this request?

FIGURE 2-6: Data from Google's Gemini.

REMEMBER

These examples are in no way meant to suggest one AI tool spews out errors and the others don't or one is more complete than the others. It simply occurred in these particular instances. Just remember that AI tools are susceptible to inconsistencies and inaccurate information. As you journey through this book, you'll come to appreciate the significance of WI.

Playing with the Pros

Comprehensive proposal-writing tools for professional users can help to streamline the application process by providing templates, guidance on writing compelling proposals, budget planning features, and sometimes even access to databases of grant opportunities. These tools can save time, enhance organization, and improve the quality of grant applications, increasing the likelihood of securing funding for projects. You can find out more about them in the nearby sidebar, "Knowing the difference between a chatbot and a comprehensive AI tool." Some of the tools are free; some are for a fee.

In addition to simplifying the application process, these tools often offer features such as deadline reminders, collaboration capabilities for team-based proposals, and analytics to track progress and success rates. They may also provide access to resources such as sample proposals, grant-writing tips, and databases of funding sources tailored to specific fields or regions. By leveraging these tools effectively, professionals can optimize their grant-seeking efforts, identify suitable funding opportunities, and craft compelling proposals that resonate with funders.

AI
SPOTLIGHT

If you're ready to join the big leagues and play with the pros, here are some comprehensive grant-writing AI tools to consider:

>> **AmpliFund:** https://www.amplifund.com

>> **Blackbaud:** https://www.blackbaud.com

>> **Grantable:** https://www.grantable.co

>> **Optimy:** https://www.optimy.com/grant-management-solution

>> **Rqawards:** https://rqawards.com/grants

>> **Submittable:** https://www.submittable.com

KNOWING THE DIFFERENCE BETWEEN A CHATBOT AND A COMPREHENSIVE AI TOOL

Chatbot and comprehensive AI tools are both AI applications, but they differ in their capabilities and scope.

Chatbot

A *chatbot* is a software program that simulates human conversation and interacts with users through a chat interface. It's designed to understand and respond to queries or commands in a conversational way. Chatbots are found across various communication channels, such as websites, messaging apps, or voice assistants. Here are some key characteristics of a chatbot:

- **Simulating human conversation:** Provides a natural language interface (NLF) for users to interact with.

- **Task-specific:** Handles specific tasks or provides information within a defined domain.

- **Rule-based or AI-powered:** Follows predefined decision trees, using techniques such as NLP and machine learning to understand and generate responses.

Comprehensive AI Tool

A *comprehensive AI tool* is more robust, such as those listed in the section "Playing with the Pros." The term refers to an all-embracing software platform that incorporates advanced AI capabilities to perform complex tasks or solve more sophisticated problems. These tools often leverage machine learning, deep learning, and other AI techniques to provide advanced functionalities. Here are some key characteristics of a comprehensive AI tool:

- **Advanced capabilities:** Performs complex tasks such as image recognition, natural language understanding, predictive analytics, or autonomous decision-making.

- **Data-driven:** Employs large datasets to learn patterns, make predictions, or generate insights.

- **Customizability:** Can be customized or trained on specific data-sets to adapt to specific business needs or domains.

- **Scalability:** Designed to handle large-scale data processing and analysis, making them suitable for enterprise-level applications.

In summary, while a chatbot focuses on simulating human conversation and providing specific information or performing tasks within a defined domain, a comprehensive AI tool encompasses a broader range of advanced AI capabilities and is designed to tackle more complex issues.

Choosing the AI Tool That's "Write" for You

When choosing an AI grant-writing tool, here are a few key factors to consider:

>> **Ease of use:** Some tools are complex and use confusing steps and different templates to generate even the simplest pieces of content. Look for user-friendly interfaces and comprehensive tutorials.

>> **Type of content:** Consider the type of content you're looking to create. Different AI writing tools specialize in various kinds of content, so it's crucial to find one that fits your needs. Do you need a content generator, a summarizer, or a language translator (to name just a few functions)?

>> **Language model:** Choose an AI writing tool that uses the best language models. At the time of writing, systems such as ChatGPT that are powered by OpenAI GPT-4 are the most advanced, but others are closing in fast.

>> **Language used:** Make sure the AI writing tool you choose can understand and write in your writing style and language. Some AI tools write in English only, while others can write perfect copy in hundreds of commonly used languages.

>> **Original content:** Original content is vital. Make sure the AI writing tool you choose is capable of producing unique, original content.

>> **Pricing:** Although prices vary among providers (and many tools are free), evaluate the tool's features and capabilities to ensure it meets your specific needs and goals.

WARNING

Caveat emptor (buyer beware)! One of the quirks of AI is that without a little human wizardry, it can sometimes lead you astray. It might not always deliver spot-on data and could send you paddling into some murky waters. So, always play detective — double-check everything and keep your radar up for consistency and accuracy!

Chapter **3**

Winning Hearts and Minds of Funders through Storytelling

A t its core, storytelling is about connections. It allows us to see the world from another perspective, stirring empathy and inspiring action. When you're seeking funding, storytelling can transform a grant proposal from a boring, dry document into a persuasive narrative that speaks to grant reviewers — appealing to their hearts and opening their wallets.

People have been sharing stories since the beginning of time. A cave painting found on an Indonesian island (dating back 45,000 years) is thought to be the earliest known record of storytelling. It depicts a pig and buffalo hunt, mythological figures in a hunting scene. Hand gestures told stories before there were words. Thousands of years later Aesop's fables started capturing imaginations and still teach valuable lessons. From the early bards, to Middle-Ages troubadours, to chart-topping books and Hollywood blockbusters, we all enjoy a good story.

As you read through this chapter, you'll uncover why stories are the hidden gems of a killer grant proposal. Get ready to learn how AI can help you to spin narratives that tug at heartstrings and loosen purse strings.

SHERYL SAYS

Understanding Why Stories Make a Difference

When it comes to grant reviewers, understanding the human brain is key. The brain's inherent affinity for stories means that proposals containing compelling narratives are more likely to capture attention and leave a lasting impression. Rather than just presenting dry data and objectives, framing your grant proposal as a story — complete with a clear beginning, middle, and end — can help reviewers connect emotionally and intellectually with your project.

By weaving your goals, challenges, and potential impacts into a narrative, you make your proposal not only more engaging but also more memorable. This approach leverages the power of storytelling to make your case more persuasive and relatable, increasing your chances of a thumbs up.

Once the reviewers are engaged, take them on the journey with stories that grab attention, evoke their imagination, create empathy, link human experiences, change beliefs, maintain interest, and persuade.

Each story should have a point to grasp and identify with. It's like painting a picture, something to visualize what happened at a particular time or place to people just like them. Every story should fit within the context of your grant proposal to support what you want your reviewer to think, feel, or learn.

REMEMBER

Using AI as Your Assistant to Crafting Engaging Stories

Here are some AI tools worth checking out to assist with your storytelling:

>> **ChatGPT:** https://chatgpt.com

>> **Copy.ai:** https://www.copy.ai

>> **Jasper:** https://www.jasper.ai

>> **NovelAI:** https://novelai.net

>> **Rytr:** https://rytr.me

>> **Scalenut:** https://www.scalenut.com

>> **Squibler:** https://www.squibler.io

>> **StoryLab.ai:** https://storylab.ai

>> **Writesonic:** https://writesonic.com

Using Prompts to Write Stories

You can feed an AI tool with prompts or specific details and it will spew out stories that can persuade and share your call to action, which is the "pot of gold." Chapter 5 is your gateway to writing skillful prompts. Whether your intent is to persuade a grantor to fund your project or persuade a donor to fund your emerging business, you need to create a strong case. For example, your prompt may read:

> *I'm applying for a grant. Create a compelling story about [details] that will tug at funder's heartstrings. Create fictitious names and places.*

Here's a great tip: Incorporating a story at the beginning of your proposal (and throughout as needed for emphasis) is a very powerful strategy for capturing the attention of the reviewers early on. You can create a memorable and impactful impression when you draw on real-life examples and anecdotes that highlight the project's relevance and potential.

In each of the following examples, I provided ChatGPT with factual prompts and the tone I wanted to create. The chatbot transformed these facts into poignant stories. It's worth noting that each of these proposals successfully secured the funding that was requested. (While the stories themselves didn't directly secure the funding, they undoubtedly played a crucial role in shaping a positive initial impression.)

An example of a grant for a community project:

> **Prompt:** *In [city] a $250,000 grant was used to transform a run-down 5-story building into a community center. 75 teens painted the walls with 10 colorful murals, there are 3 art workshops, and 2 music rooms. Upon completion, the teens participated in art projects, poetry slams, and theaters performances drawing in over 100 people. It was a very positive experience for everyone. Make this story more interesting and limit it to two paragraphs.*

> **AI's response:** *In [city], a group of 75 teenagers found hope and opportunity when a generous grant of $250,000 transformed an abandoned 5-story building into a vibrant community center. Walls that were once cold and lifeless now adorn 10 colorful murals painted by some of the teens — a reflection of the creativity that now flourishes within. With 2 dance studios, 3 art workshops, and 2 music rooms at their disposal, these once-overlooked, troubled teens discovered their talents and found their voices.*

> *Through art projects, poetry slams, and theater performances, these teens have captivated their community, drawing in an audience of over 100 people, and they're now participants in shaping their own futures. The funding not only repurposed a derelict building, but it lit a brighter future for these inner city teens, empowering them to strive and thrive.*

An example of a grant for medical research:

> **Prompt:** *As a result of a prior grant, 300 patients participated in a program that allowed researchers to explore the complexities of coronary artery disease, heart failure, and arrhythmias. These 300 patients who once faced a bleak future now have reason to hope for a prolonged life. Bring more life to this story and tug at the reader's heartstrings. Make it brief.*

AI's response: *Imagine being diagnosed with a life-threatening condition, where every breath feels like a struggle, and every heartbeat is a reminder of your mortality. For 300 patients in this study, the last round of grant funding paved the way for ground-breaking medical research. It brought hope and a renewed sense of life to these patients suffering from coronary artery disease, heart failure, and arrhythmias.*

The grant money has allowed researchers to dive deep into the complexities of these diseases, exploring innovative approaches and pushing the boundaries of medical knowledge. This level of dedication and commitment has not only resulted in improved patient outcomes but has also opened doors to new possibilities in the field of cardiology. These 300 patients who were once facing a bleak prognosis now have access to life-prolonging therapies that were once only dreams. These therapies have not only reduced mortality rates but have significantly enhanced the quality of life for these patients and their families.

Through our partnership, we can illuminate a path of optimism, making inhaling a rejuvenating experience for people seeking the simple joy of effortless breathing.

An example of a grant to help inner–city women:

Prompt: *Add more drama to this: In [city] 5 women shared a vision to empower inner-city women through education, leading to entrepreneurship. With a $150,000 grant they provided free vocational training in coding, graphic design, and culinary arts. They also established mentorship programs where professional woman offered guidance and support to these women. As a result, 50 women who were once living in poverty have started their own businesses. And they paid it forward. Many of them now serve as mentors to entirely new groups of women. They have become beacon of hope for other women who want to follow in their footsteps.*

AI's response: *In the heart of the bustling [city], five passionate and determined women came together with a shared vision to uplift their community. With the help of a generous grant of $150,000, they launched a project aimed at empowering inner-city women through education and entrepreneurship. The project provided free vocational training in fields such as coding, graphic* *design, and culinary arts, giving these women the skills to pursue meaningful careers and break the cycle of poverty. Additionally, the grant enabled the creation of a mentorship program, where successful female professionals from the community offered guidance and support to the participants, fostering a strong network of empowerment and encouragement. As the months passed, the impact of the project became evident. Fifty women who had once felt trapped by their circumstances were now thriving in their chosen fields. Many have started their own businesses and are becoming role models for the next generation, in addition to becoming mentors to the next group of women.*

The project's success extended beyond individual achievements, as the entire community experienced a positive transformation. The grant had not only changed the lives of these women but had also sown the seeds for a brighter, more empowered future for the entire city. The project's success story became a beacon of hope, inspiring other communities to invest in similar initiatives and uplift women across the state.

Taking Reviewers on a Journey

Including stories in a grant proposal conveys the project's purpose and anticipated impact while building a compelling and emotionally engaging argument for funding. This immerses the reviewers in the journey of others which cultivates empathy, dismantles barriers, and challenges assumptions.

REMEMBER

A compelling grant narrative weaves together essential elements such as background information, project specifics, and personal anecdotes that vividly illustrate your passion and your mission. These stories should expand upon the following themes:

>> Highlighting the potential for long-term success and impact, as funders are more willing to invest in projects with a long-term perspective and scalability.

>> Demonstrating sustainability beyond the grant period and emphasize the importance of the program to the community, as well as the significance of evaluation to sustainability.

EVERY STORY HAS A HERO

Invite the grantor to partner with you on a journey so they become heroes too. Start by painting a vivid picture.

- What are the problems your funding will solve?
- What difference have you made or can you make?
- How have you solved these problems in the past?
- How can their funding make the resolution possible?
- What's the sustainability of this venture?

Quantify data where applicable with numbers of people, percentages, dollars, and so on. They're a vital part of the story.

In the following example, I used AI to consolidate this story to include as the opening in the cover letter. (Check out Chapter 8 for more on creating impactful cover letters.) Notice how it includes *together we can*, making the reviewer part of the journey:

> **Prompt:** *Add a powerful "together we can" to the story on how funding enabled researchers to pioneer groundbreaking medical advancements for 300 patients, leading to improved outcomes and life-prolonging therapies for coronary artery disease, heart failure, and arrhythmias.*

> **AI's response:** *Grant funding has enabled researchers to pioneer groundbreaking medical advancements for 300 patients, leading to improved outcomes and life-prolonging therapies for coronary artery disease, heart failure, and arrhythmias. Together we can bring optimism and the simple joy of effortless breathing to thousands of people in need.*

Creating Your Own Success Stories

By leveraging AI capabilities, you can present a more compelling and impactful case (via stories) to potential grantors. AI can assist with data analysis, personalization, visualization, and language enhancement making your stories come alive. Include in your prompts words such as *highlight, conversational, lighthearted, heartfelt, emphasize, create a hook, give an analogy, express gratitude,* or whatever is appropriate. (Chapter 5 offers loads of tips for writing compelling prompts that get you the response you want.)

>> Begin by setting the stage with a powerful introduction that grabs the reviewer's attention and piques their interest.

>> Describe the project or initiative in vivid detail, emphasizing its unique qualities and the potential it holds for making a significant difference in the targeted area or community.

>> Use evocative language to create a sense of anticipation and excitement.

>> Artfully emphasize the groundbreaking aspects of your proposal.

>> Highlight the key features or components that set your project apart and make it a game-changer in its field. Whether it's a new approach to solving a pressing social issue, a breakthrough in scientific research, or an innovative program to support underserved communities, convey the significance of your project with unwavering confidence and enthusiasm.

>> Underscore the uniqueness and potential impact of your proposal.

>> Paint a vivid picture of the transformative force it represents, setting it apart from other initiatives and illustrating how it will redefine the landscape of its respective field.

>> Express your gratitude for the opportunity to introduce this groundbreaking project to the grantor.

>> Emphasize the potential for your initiative to seamlessly integrate into the fabric of the community or field, setting new standards for innovation, impact, and positive change.

REMEMBER

By conveying a sense of profound conviction and unwavering confidence in your proposal, you can build anticipation and imagery that resonates with potential grantors.

Naming names

When showcasing the success of one or two people, avoid generic labels such as *the supervisor, the instructor,* or *the student.* Instead, include names, whether real or fictitious. (If you use real names, be sure to get written permission first.) This creates an element of personalization and relatability. It also reinforces to the grant reviewer that behind every grant request lies a human story deserving of support and investment. Here's an example generated by AI for a person seeking funding:

> **Prompt:** *Write a heartfelt story about Pete, a widowed father, working three jobs, who struggled to fund his daughter Yolanda's dream of becoming a doctor for their underserved community. With AI's help in finding grants and scholarships, Yolanda was able to pursue her medical education despite their financial hardships. Add something about "together we can."*

> **AI's response:** *In the depths of Pete's struggle as a widowed father, working three jobs, his greatest concern was providing for his daughter, Yolanda, who had dreams of becoming a family doctor in a rural community that was in much need of medical services. Despite Pete's efforts, financial limitations threatened to dash her aspirations. However, hope emerged when a community grant (discovered with the aid of AI) offered Yolanda a scholarship to pursue her dreams.*

> *This story of resilience, opportunity, and resourcefulness reminds us of the power of collective support. Through initiatives like community grants, we can empower not only all the Yolandas, but countless others like her — the Carlas, the Chens, and the Pedros — to reach their full potential. Together, we can build a community where barriers dissolve, dreams flourish, and a brighter future is cultivated for generations to come.*

Creating imaginary stories

If you don't have an actual story, create a realistic story to capture the reviewer's imagination. See how AI evokes imagination in the following example of seeking funding for research:

> **Prompt:** *Create a compelling story about a world where technology and nature collide and how funding may lead to a medical breakthrough. Tack on something about "together we can. . ."*

> **AI's response:** *Imagine a world where technology and nature collide, a group of researchers venture into an uncharted rainforest. As they explore, they find rare medicinal plants that could transform modern medicine and save lives. These plants may*

contain compounds that could be used to develop new drugs, treatments, and cures for a wide range of diseases and ailments. The exploration could lead to breakthroughs in the treatment of illnesses that currently have limited or no effective remedies, thus improving the overall health and well-being of people around the world.

With your support, the researchers can conduct vital research, document their discoveries, and bring back knowledge that could benefit humanity for years to come. This grant proposal aims to fund their expedition and pave the way for a healthier future. Together we can make this extraordinary journey of exploration, innovation, and hope a reality.

Telling before and after stories

REMEMBER

Before and after stories play a crucial role in conveying the impact and necessity of the project. These stories serve as powerful tools for communicating the significance of the project and can effectively evoke emotions and create a sense of urgency. By effectively demonstrating the transformation brought about by the project, funders can better understand the tangible outcomes and the value of their support:

Prompt: *In the small rural community of Maplewood, lack of access to education, healthcare, and economic opportunities had trapped its residents in a cycle of poverty and despair. Children walked miles to the nearest school, families struggled to afford basic healthcare, and unemployment was rampant. The community lacked infrastructure, and hope seemed like a distant dream. Create a compelling story about how a grant provided medical care, established vocational training, and empowered adults to break the cycle of poverty. State this better and call out the impact.*

AI's response:

Thanks to the generous support of our donors, the landscape of Maplewood has been transformed. A new school has been built, providing quality education to the children who once walked for miles. A healthcare center now stands at the heart of the community, offering vital medical services to families in need. With the funding provided, we've established vocational training programs, empowering adults with the skills needed to secure employment and break the cycle of poverty. The once desolate streets are now bustling with small businesses and entrepreneurial ventures, breathing new life into the community.

Impact: To put it into perspective, over 500 children in Maplewood now have access to quality education, which has not only increased their literacy rates but also opened doors to a brighter future. Additionally, more than 200 families have been able to receive essential medical care, improving their overall well-being and quality of life.

Furthermore, our programs have equipped over 300 individuals with the skills and resources they need to secure employment and build sustainable livelihoods. As a result, the once bleak outlook in Maplewood has been replaced with hope and opportunity for over 1000 people, all thanks to the generosity of donors like you.

REMEMBER

Even stories that end in disappointment can be profound sources of wisdom. Before facing their outcomes, these narratives often teach us about the importance of preparation, resilience, and adaptability. Afterward, they offer valuable insights into overcoming failure, learning from mistakes, and growing stronger from adversity. The lessons gleaned from both the journey and the outcome shape our ability to handle future challenges with greater insight and empathy.

Seeking volunteers' stories

A story in letter form from a volunteer can provide a personal, heartfelt perspective on the impact of the proposal. It showcases community support and commitment, which can significantly increase the chances of being funded. Here's an example:

Prompt: *Write an enthusiastic letter of testimony from a recipient who benefitted from funding for equipment for an after-school center. Add appropriate details that will strengthen the case. Make it somewhat formal, but not stuffy.*

AI's response:

Dear [Recipient's Name],

I am writing to offer my enthusiastic support for the grant proposal to secure funding for gym and outdoor equipment for our after-school center. As a dedicated volunteer at the center for the past two years, I've witnessed firsthand the positive impact that physical activity and outdoor play will have on the children in our community.

When the children first arrive after a long day at school, I often see them filled with restless energy. However, once we are able to take them outside for games of tag or soccer, I notice their mood shift dramatically. They're laughing, smiling, and interacting with each other in healthy ways. Being active outside allows them to burn off steam in a constructive manner.

I have also noticed that the children seem more focused during quiet homework and craft activities that follow outdoor time. Getting exercise and fresh air improves both their concentration and behavior. Many parents have commented to me privately about how much calmer and happier their children are on days they are able to play outside after school versus days spent cooped up indoors.

The acquisition of gym and outdoor equipment, such as balls, hula hoops, and climbing structures, would enhance the benefits the children currently receive from outdoor time. It will allow them to engage in more organized sports and activities led by our staff. This equipment will contribute greatly to the physical, mental and social-emotional wellbeing of the children in our care.

I strongly urge you to support this grant proposal. The impact of this funding would be immeasurable in both the short and long-term.

Sincerely,

[Your Name]

After-School Volunteer

Preparing case studies

Case studies help illustrate real-world scenarios, develop problem-solving skills, and provide practical insights by analyzing specific examples and their outcomes. Think of case studies as the juicy anecdotes in a gripping novel — they add depth, relatability, and real-world impact to your grant proposal. When you weave a compelling case study into your proposal, you're essentially bringing your project to life. You're showing the funder, "This isn't just a theoretical idea; it's something that's already making a difference in people's lives." So, next time you're drafting a grant proposal, don't forget to sprinkle in some captivating case studies.

Use the AI tools mentioned earlier in this chapter to help generate compelling case studies. They can organize information and provide structure, ensuring the case studies effectively highlight the impact of your project. Here's an example about empowering youth through digital literacy:

Prompt: *Create a compelling story about 16-year-old Emily who joined a Digital Literacy Program at YEI. She had no computers to use. A grant helped her gain confidence and do better in school, and now she's aiming for a tech career. Show how the program made a difference to Emily and other students like her.*

AI's response: *In a rural community with limited educational resources, Emily, a 16-year-old student, lacked access to computer science opportunities until she joined our Digital Literacy Program at Youth Empowerment Initiative (YEI). With our support, Emily gained access to computers and mentorship, quickly developing coding and graphic design skills. This newfound proficiency boosted Emily's confidence and academic performance and inspired her to pursue a career in technology, which would have otherwise been unavailable to her.*

Emily's success underscores the impact of our programs in bridging the digital divide for underserved youths. Together our grant can expand these transformative opportunities to more students like Emily, empowering them for future success.

Embellishing Stories

Gandalf, a hero in J.R.R. Tolkien's *The Hobbit*, advised Bilbo Baggins that embellishing his tales upon returning from his adventure would make them more captivating. This advice resonates beyond literature; embellishment enhances storytelling across various artistic realms. Choreographers refine dance compositions by adding subtle gestures and movements to evoke emotion, while musical arrangers enrich scores with trills and passing tones without straying from the original melody. Similarly, movie scripts often take liberties with true events to heighten drama and audience connection (as seen in the fictional characters of Jack and Rose in the movie *Titanic*, who humanized the historical tragedy).

In your own storytelling, incorporating embellishments such as metaphors, humor, or vivid details can transform a narrative from mundane to memorable. By focusing on conflict or any strong emotion or plotline, you can engage reviewers and evoke genuine emotional responses, leveraging creative freedom to craft narratives that resonate long after they're read or heard.

SHERYL SAYS

I understand that suggesting embellishment may be controversial, but effectively drawing your reviewer into the story can enhance engagement. You can do it without sacrificing the story's authenticity by elaborating on the setting, characters, clothing, feelings, reactions, and more.

AI SPOTLIGHT

AI tools, such as those mentioned earlier in this chapter, can embellish stories by using detailed and specific prompts to extend and add more detail to sentences, role-play as a prompt generator for a specific AI tool, refine answers as more information is added, and compose sonnets, write code, get philosophical, and automate tasks. To prompt chatbots effectively, it's important to provide clear and concise language, include examples of what is or isn't expected, and specify the format or structure of the response (find out more in Chapter 5).

Additionally, providing context and specific details, such as tone of voice, style, and examples of interactions, can help elicit the desired type of response from chatbots. To embellish stories effectively, prompts should be specific and detailed. Some prompt ideas that can be used to generate story embellishments include:

>> Ask the chatbot to extend and add more detail to sentences, such as *Could you expand this story by adding more details and examples to make it more engaging and vivid?*

>> Prompt the chatbot to refine its answers as more and more information is added. Here's an example: *As I provide more information, continuously refine and adjust your responses to better fit the new details.*

>> Specify to the chatbot the format or structure of the response, such as asking for a short story or brief description. Here's a prompt for this: *Could you provide your response in the form of a short story or a brief description, depending on what best suits the content?*

SHARING STORIES IN THE FIRST PERSON, PRESENT TENSE

Punctuate your story by telling it in the first person, present tense. This creates real-time immediacy, a sense of urgency. It gives the reader the feeling of plunging into the situation with you.

Present tense (first person): *As I walk onto the stage to make my presentation to the reviewing panel, I feel the anticipation in the air. Suddenly, there's a power failure. My mind races, trying to think of a quick solution.*

Past tense (third person): *Kate walked onto the stage confidently, but moments later there was a power failure that plunged the room into darkness. She stood bewildered, unsure of her next move.*

The present-tense scenario in first person amplifies the intensity. The reading or listening audience puts themselves in the shoes of that person, pondering, "What would I do?"

>> Provide context and specific details for the chatbot to use, such as tone of voice, style, and examples of interactions. Include words such a *fun, formal, first person, active voice,* and so on.

Using AI tools to enhance stories ensures consistency and creativity while maintaining the story's authenticity.

WARNING

Embellishing stories by adding fanciful details isn't lying, provided it's grounded in reality. But you must know where to draw the line between adding fanciful details and being dishonest.

Preparing Strong Headlines That Tell a Story

Newspapers and magazines leverage impactful headlines to visually entice their readers. When you craft strong, compelling headlines, grant reviewers can quickly skim through your grant proposals and grasp essential information at a glance, even if they lack time to delve into the full document. Including pertinent numbers further enhances the proposal's credibility. Here are several illustrative examples of informative and uninformative headlines:

> **Informative headline:** *Empowering 10,000 Youths with Job Skills Training*

> **Uninformative headline:** *Empowering Youths*

> **Informative headline:** *Measurable outcome: Reducing carbon emissions by 20% in the first year through the implementation of energy-efficient systems in local schools.*

> **Uninformative headline:** *Measurable outcome*

> **Informative headline:** *Timeline: Constructing 5 new community centers within the next 18 months.*

> **Uninformative headline:** *Timeline*

REMEMBER

A one-line story (such as a headline) can be a powerful storytelling tool, packing a punch of emotion, imagery, or intrigue into just a few words. When well crafted, this single line can leave a lasting impression and spark the reviewer's imagination.

AI SPOTLIGHT

If you need help generating headlines, turn to your favorite chatbot for help (as I did for many headings throughout this book). Figure 3-1 shows a few informative headline examples from ChatGPT that tell a story.

ChatGPT

"Accelerating Impact: Achieving Milestones 20% Faster with a Streamlined Timeline"

"Maximizing Resources: Delivering Results Within Budget - Saving 15% on Project Costs"

"Sustainable Solutions: Reducing Environmental Footprint by 25% Through Innovative Practices"

"Expertise at the Helm: Leveraging 50 Years of Combined Experience for Project Success"

FIGURE 3-1: AI-generated headlines that tell a story.

Each of these one-liners hints at a larger narrative, inviting the grant reviewer to fill in the details and around the brief but evocative scenario. A good one-liner can be open to interpretation while still conveying a complete emotional arc or pivotal moment. Despite their brevity, these examples demonstrate how a single line can prompt the mind to imagine the rest of the story and drive your proposal to the top of the pile.

Incorporating Visual Storytelling

In today's fast-paced world, mastering communication is essential. While words are powerful, adding savvy visuals acts like rocket boosters — elevating your message's impact. This is especially true for grant proposals, where well-designed visuals can simplify complex data and make your case more compelling and memorable to reviewers.

Picture this: You're diving into a grant proposal. It's a total text tsunami, drowning in details. Even the most dedicated reviewer might start seeing double, missing the gems hidden within. Now imagine the same proposal, but this time, it's sprinkled with a dash of diagrams, tables and charts. Suddenly, those complex concepts aren't so intimidating; they're enlightening and understandable.

REMEMBER

Graphics can unravel intricate processes, shine a spotlight on crucial connections, and serve up those brain-bending ideas on a silver platter of clarity and precision. Also, visuals don't play favorites with languages. They're the ultimate polyglots, breaking down barriers, boosting comprehension, and giving your proposal that extra oomph it needs to stand out from the crowd. So, when in doubt about clarity, let your visuals do the talking.

When skillfully integrated, graphics become an integral part of the visual storytelling process, guiding the reviewer through the proposal's journey and reinforcing key messages along the way. Graphics can elevate a grant proposal by visually communicating complex ideas and data in a clear, concise manner. Well-designed visuals act as powerful storytelling tools that reinforce key points and enhance the overall narrative, visually communicating complex ideas and data clearly and concisely.

To enhance your proposal, try out the following ideas:

>> Use diagrams and flowcharts to illustrate processes, methodologies, or project timelines in an easy-to-follow format.

>> Incorporate charts and graphs to present quantitative data, trends, or statistics in a visually compelling way.

>> Include maps, blueprints, or architectural renderings to provide spatial context for location-based projects.

>> Include a table to show the breakdown of the budget.

>> Include graphics in the executive summary when appropriate.

Without trying to sound too self-serving (okay, maybe just a little), my book *Business Writing with AI For Dummies* (John Wiley & Sons, Inc., 2024) goes into a lot of detail about using visuals for storytelling. It's worth checking out.

Using AI as your assistant to create dynamic visuals

You don't need to be a graphic designer with fancy software to create pleasing-looking visuals for grant proposals. When it comes to images, AI certainly struts its stuff. Here are some of the popular AI tools for creating visual aids:

>> **Adobe Photoshop:** https://www.adobe.com

>> **Adobe Sensei:** https://www.adobe.com/sensei

>> **Alpaca:** https://www.alpacaml.com

>> **AutoDraw:** https://www.autodraw.com

>> **DALL-E:** https://openai.com/index/dall-e

>> **Deep Art Effects:** https://www.deeparteffects.com

>> **Designs.ai:** https://designs.ai/en

>> **Jasper.ai:** https://www.jasper.ai

>> **Khroma:** https://www.khroma.co

>> **LetsEnhance:** https://letsenhance.io

>> **Lucidchart:** https://www.lucidchart.com/pages

>> **Nvidia Canvas:** https://www.nvidia.com/en-us/studio/canvas

>> **Uizard:** https://uizard.io

Also, ChatGPT (https://chatgpt.com) offers various plugins such as WebPilot Plugin and Show Me Diagrams that can be used to create graphs and visualizations.

Going beyond graphics

Think of visuals in the broader sense. Anything the reader sees is a *visual*, not just a graphic. Visual impact organizes information into manageable, bite-sized chunks of information, making it easy to read. It also emphasizes what's important by separating major points from minor points. Non-graphic visuals bring life to your content by strategically using white space, fonts, punchy lists, dynamic paragraph and sentence lengths, and captivating headlines. Therefore:

>> Leave 1" margins on the top, bottom, and sides.

>> Limit paragraphs to about eight lines of text.

>> Double space between paragraphs.

>> Limit sentences to no more than 20 words.

>> Include descriptive headlines and subheadings.

**AI
SPOTLIGHT**

Using AI tools can assist in organizing content effectively and ensuring readability by suggesting optimal paragraph lengths, sentence structures, and headline creation.

2

Prepping for Your Proposal

Unlock the grant-writing Kick-Start Brief — your ultimate game-changer for crafting proposals that instantly wow grant reviewers and make them sit up and take notice!

Master the art of writing AI prompts that not only get you spot-on answers but also make your chatbot think, "Whoa, I can't wait to respond to this!"

Discover how AI can spotlight keywords like tiny beacons, helping your grant proposal shine brightly through even the toughest review processes.

Turn a blank page into a playground of creativity with AI transforming your ideas into a masterpiece of possibilities.

Chapter **4**

Scoping the Proposal with a Kick-Start Brief

Before diving into the grant proposal–writing process, it's crucial to get into the minds of the folks who'll be reading them — the grant reviewers. They start with the cover letter, which is like the proposal's first impression. If it piques their interest, they move on to the title page, then to the executive summary. (Unlock more about these topics in Part 3.) If they pass muster, the reviewer will give the rest of the proposal a closer look.

SHERYL SAYS

This is where a Kick-Start Brief steps in. It's your stealth tool for structuring and presenting your proposal. By following it you can develop a connection with the reviewers, help them understand why your project matters, and turn your ideas into a compelling case for funding.

Kick-Starting Your Proposal

As an experienced grant proposal writer, I never commit one word to my computer until I've completed a *Kick-Start Brief*. This is a critical part of the proposal–writing process because it sets the foundation for a well-structured proposal. It ensures all stakeholders have a shared understanding and expectations are aligned, which helps in streamlining the development process, avoiding misunderstandings and increasing the likelihood of successful outcomes. By addressing these before you start writing, you can identify potential challenges and resources needed, making the entire proposal more focused and actionable.

REMEMBER

The Kick-Start Brief is shown in Figure 4-1. Print it out and keep it handy. Use it as it appears or amend it to suit your proposal. Go ahead and fill out your answers to the questions it poses — simply dive in and get started! This not only saves you time and effort in the long-term but also increases the clarity and impact of your proposal, putting you in a stronger position to attract support and reach your goals more effectively.

Grant Writing Kick-Start Brief

1. What is the problem statement?

2. Does this overlap another grant (internal perhaps)? If so, what makes your request different?

3. What are your specific needs? (Remember you should follow the needs, not the money).

4. What is your goal? (State in one sentence.)

5. What are your objectives?

   • Short- and long-term?

   • How will you measure success?

6. What are your budgetary needs?

7. What's the timeline?

8. What's the sustainability?

9. What are your plans for promoting the program?

10. Who is your target population?

11. What are the best practices?

12. Who is your reader?

13. Is anyone else in your organization seeking funding for complementary projects?

14. Why is your organization more qualified than others to do _____ ?

15. What's the one *key point* you want your readers to remember?

FIGURE 4-1: A Kick-Start Brief for grant writers.

SHERYL SAYS

When I introduce the Kick-Start Brief at my grant proposal-writing workshops, I often hear participants lament about their jam-packed schedules and wonder how they'll find the time to use it. But here's the twist: After giving it a whirl and drafting a chunk of their proposal during the workshop, they're usually amazed at how they ever managed without it. Many let me know later on about slashing their grant-writing time by 30 to 50 percent and snagging more funding to boot. Give it a go and see if you can achieve the same stellar results!

Finding Nuggets in the Numbers with AI

The following sections look at each question on the Kick-Start Brief in more detail (the numbers match up to the questions in Figure 4-1).

AI SPOTLIGHT

Once you've answered the key questions posed on the Kick-Start Brief, just plug the information into your chatbot and watch the magic unfold. The chatbot can take your detailed input and turn it into a polished proposal with ease. For more on how AI can streamline this process and make your life easier, check out the details towards the end of this chapter.

1. What is the problem statement?

The *problem statement* forms the cornerstone of the entire proposal, defining the specific issue that the project seeks to address with funding. It should succinctly describe the problem's significance, scope, and potential consequences if left unresolved. This involves identifying key obstacles, such as limited access to nutritious food or high poverty rates that necessitate intervention.

To bolster credibility, the statement should reference relevant research, data, or community assessments that originally identified the problem's extent and causes. Additionally, it should emphasize the urgency of action by outlining the negative impacts on individuals, communities, or society as a whole by not addressing this problem. This approach underscores the need for funding to mitigate these consequences effectively. (You'll find an example of a problem statement in Chapter 12.)

AI can play a key role in creating a strong problem statement by analyzing data to identify core issues. It can review research, community assessments, and statistics to highlight the problem's significance and urgency. AI helps craft a clear narrative by automating the synthesis of information, making the case for funding and intervention more compelling.

2. Does this overlap another grant? What makes your request different?

When considering the overlap with another grant, this can have implications for resource allocation, project coordination, and the overall impact of the proposed initiative. Be transparent about any potential overlap and clearly communicate how the current request differs from existing grants, if any. This may involve highlighting unique aspects of the proposed project, such as its innovative approach, specific target beneficiaries, or the distinct outcomes it aims to achieve.

AI can help you identify overlaps in grant applications, but it's not always perfect. It might assist with text comparisons, database checks, plagiarism detection, and keyword matching — so always use your writer intelligence (WI) too.

3. What are your specific needs?

In essence, following the needs not the money means developing the proposal based on identified community or organizational needs rather than tailoring it solely to match available funding opportunities or trends. It ensures that the proposed activities and goals are grounded in addressing real issues and achieving meaningful impact, rather than being driven primarily by financial considerations.

AI can address specific needs by analyzing data to identify key issues, generating insights and recommendations, and tailoring content to address the concerns of stakeholders. It helps streamline research, enhance clarity, and ensures that the proposal effectively targets and meets the identified needs.

4. What is your goal?

Goals are like your North Star, helping you focus on the path towards achieving your purpose. Even though goals may not have their own separate section in your proposal, they influence every aspect of the proposal, ensuring coherence and alignment throughout.

Here's a step-by-step process to help you craft a precise goal statement:

1. **Identify the specific SMART (specific, measurable, achievable, relevant, and time-bound) goal.** Begin by clearly defining the primary objective or outcome that you aim to achieve through the proposed project.

2. **Focus on impact.** Emphasize the intended impact or change that your project seeks to bring about. Consider the broader significance of your goal and how it aligns with the overarching mission or objectives of your organization.

3. **Be concise.** Keep your goal statement concise and to the point. Avoid unnecessary complexity or ambiguity by using clear and straightforward language that can be easily understood by reviewers. Always ask your chatbot to make your wording concise!

4. **Use action-oriented language.** Frame your goal statement using action-oriented language that conveys a sense of purpose and intentionality. Use verbs that denote action and progress, such as *to improve, to increase,* or *to reduce.* (Check out Chapter 5 to help prompt your way to success.)

5. **Include key components.** Ensure that your goal statement includes all key components necessary to convey the essence of your goal. This may include the target population or beneficiaries, the specific outcome or change you aim to achieve, and any relevant contextual information.

6. **Review and refine.** Once you have drafted your goal statement, review it carefully to ensure that it accurately reflects your intended goal and aligns with the overall focus of your proposal. Revise as needed to enhance clarity and precision. For example:

   Original goal: *To improve access to healthcare services for underserved communities.*

   Refined goal: *The goal is to increase access to primary healthcare services for low-income families in rural areas by establishing mobile clinics and community health outreach programs.*

AI tools can help refine your goal statement by suggesting concise and impactful language, ensuring it aligns with SMART criteria and resonates with reviewers.

5. What are your objectives?

Objectives encompass both short-term and long-term goals, each playing a crucial role in guiding the project's implementation and measuring its success:

>> **Short-term objectives** are achievable milestones that might involve immediate actions such as conducting a market analysis, piloting a product, or training staff for project implementation.

>> **Long-term objectives** focus on broader impacts such as expanding market reach, achieving significant revenue growth, or establishing a dominant position in the industry.

AI aids in setting long- and short-term objectives in a proposal by analyzing historical data to identify successful strategies and predicting outcomes for various objectives. It can align goals with organizational priorities, suggest realistic timelines and resource allocations, and monitor progress to allow for timely adjustments. This ensures more informed and strategic goal setting.

6. What are your budgetary needs?

Provide a detailed *budget* that breaks down all anticipated costs, including direct costs (such as personnel, materials, travel), indirect costs (overhead, facilities), and any equipment or other expenses. Ensure the budget aligns with the funding agency's requirements and limitations, such as restrictions on certain expense categories or caps on total funding. Be sure to

>> Explain and justify each budget line item, including how the costs were calculated. Provide supporting documentation where relevant.

>> Account for any required cost-sharing or matching funds from your organization.

>> Factor in applicable taxes, fringe benefits, and indirect/ overhead costs, and get approval from your institution's grant administration office.

>> Present the budget in a clear, organized format, such as a spreadsheet or table, to make it easy for reviewers to understand.

AI can whip up a budget breakdown in table format that's a breeze to breeze through, making it a snap to scan and giving the reviewer's eyes a break from the wall of text. (If you peek at Chapter 13, you'll see how visuals play an important part of connecting with the reviewers.)

7. What's the timeline?

A clear and realistic timeline is crucial for showing a project's feasibility and reassuring funders of effective resource use. A *timeline* outlines activities, milestones, and deadlines from start to finish, breaking the project into manageable phases. The timeline should also address task dependencies and potential risks, demonstrating careful planning and enhancing the proposal's credibility.

AI can assist by automating task scheduling, predicting potential delays, optimizing resources, and adjusting for changes.

8. What's the sustainability?

Addressing sustainability is vital in any grant proposal as it shows a commitment to the project's long-term impact beyond the funding period. To ensure continuity, outline plans for securing additional resources, forming partnerships, and implementing measures for ongoing success. Securing extra funding can involve diversifying sources such as government grants, corporate sponsors, individual donors, or foundations. Proactive fundraising and financial management will enhance your ability to sustain the program. Building strategic partnerships with organizations, community groups, or government agencies can also boost sustainability by leveraging resources, expertise, and networks, offering additional funding, in-kind support, and volunteer assistance.

Consider strategies for scaling or replicating the program, such as documenting best practices, developing training materials, and providing technical support. Transitioning leadership to local stakeholders can further ensure the program's continued success and relevance by fostering community ownership and building local capacity.

AI can enhance sustainability findings by using predictive analytics to identify funding opportunities, optimizing resource allocation, analyzing data to refine strategies, aiding in scalable solutions, and automating administrative tasks for greater efficiency.

9. What are your plans for promoting the program?

Promotion may include digital marketing efforts, social media campaigns, website optimization, and targeted digital advertising to raise awareness and drive engagement. Community outreach strategies might include hosting informational events, workshops, and networking opportunities to connect with key stakeholders and potential beneficiaries. Additionally, forming strategic partnerships with local organizations, businesses, and influencers can amplify the initiative's reach and impact, fostering a collaborative network of support and advocacy.

AI can provide a host of ideas that may include social media campaigns, email marketing campaigns, influencer partnerships, and more. (Check out Chapter 12 to see this in action.)

10. Who is your target population?

Provide a clear and detailed description of the *target population* that includes demographic information such as age range, gender, ethnicity, income level, education, and any special needs or considerations. This demonstrates a nuanced understanding of the community or constituency you aim to serve and ensure that the proposed project aligns closely with their needs and priorities.

For example, if you're proposing a project aimed at improving healthcare access for low-income families in a specific neighborhood, define the target population by income level, family size, and health conditions. Include demographic data and account for cultural and linguistic diversity to ensure the interventions are responsive and accessible. This might involve offering services in multiple languages and incorporating cultural preferences into the program design.

AI tools can help gather and analyze demographic data, ensuring that the description of the target population is comprehensive and data-driven. AI can also assist in tailoring the proposal to address the specific needs and preferences of the target population.

11. What are the best practices?

Best practices are methods and techniques that are widely recognized as effective and efficient in creating, organizing, and presenting a grant proposal. They may include any of the following:

>> Stating the problem or need and provide data to demonstrate it.

>> Outlining specific, measurable objectives and a detailed project plan that aligns with your budget.

>> Demonstrating your organization's experience and qualifications to carry out the proposed project.

>> Explaining how you will sustain the project beyond the grant period and incorporate matching funds or other funding sources. Defining success metrics for your project, including both outputs and outcomes.

12. Who is your reader?

Grant proposals are screened electronically for completeness and eligibility and/or by experts in the relevant field. These reviewers assess proposals based on scientific merit, feasibility, impact, and alignment with funding goals. Decisions are made based on these evaluations and any additional priorities set by the funding agency. In some cases, there may be multiple stages of review, with different levels of scrutiny applied at each stage. Ultimately, decisions about funding are made based on the evaluations provided by these reviewers, along with any additional considerations or priorities set by the funding agency.

AI SPOTLIGHT

AI tools can optimize the initial submission to ensure it meets formatting and eligibility criteria, increasing the likelihood of passing electronic screening.

13. Is anyone else in your organization seeking funding for complementary projects?

When multiple projects within the same organization are seeking funding for complementary initiatives, it's important to explore opportunities for collaboration, resource sharing, and joint initiatives.

By working together, you can maximize their impact, optimize resource utilization, and demonstrate a unified approach to addressing shared goals and priorities. This not only enhances the credibility and competitiveness of grant proposals but also fosters a culture of collaboration and innovation within the organization.

14. Why is your organization more qualified than others to do _____?

By effectively communicating why your organization is uniquely qualified to undertake the proposed initiative, you can strengthen your grant proposal and increase your chances of securing funding. This provides an opportunity to showcase your organization's strengths, expertise, and potential for making a meaningful difference in the lives of those you serve.

Consider highlighting your

>> Track record

>> Innovative approach

>> Collaborative networks

>> Potential impact

>> Future plans

>> Patents, publications, speaking engagements

>> Stories and testimonials

AI SPOTLIGHT

AI tools can help compile and analyze data on your organization's past achievements, innovative approaches, and collaborative networks, presenting a compelling case for why your organization is uniquely qualified.

15. What's the one key point you want your readers to remember?

Crafting a compelling key point is crucial for making your proposal memorable and impactful. It's essential to ensure that your core message resonates with reviewers and sticks in their minds long after they've finished reading your proposal. It's like an *earworm* (a song you hear that you can't get out of your head; it just keeps playing over and over).

Here are some handy tips for creating effective key points:

>> Present your key point clearly and simply, avoiding jargon.

>> Ensure it aligns with the grant's objectives and priorities.

>> Highlight what sets your project apart, such as innovative approaches or proven success.

>> Emphasize the tangible benefits and outcomes of your project.

>> Create a memorable hook — such as a striking statistic or anecdote — that resonates with reviewers.

>> Reflect your mission and values to reinforce credibility and commitment.

AI SPOTLIGHT

AI tools can suggest impactful and concise wording that resonates and sticks.

Using AI as Your Virtual Assistant

AI SPOTLIGHT

Once you've filled out a Kick-Start Brief, let AI be your virtual assistant in various aspects of writing your grant proposal. Here are some functions where AI can provide assistance:

>> **Writing the draft.** Write a prompt with the basic information. Your chatbot will write the draft for you and identify keywords. (Learn more about writing prompts in Chapter 5 and keywords in Chapter 6.)

>> **Data analysis and research.** AI can help researchers analyze large datasets quickly and efficiently, identifying trends, patterns, and correlations relevant to the grant proposal's objectives.

>> **Literature review.** AI-powered tools can assist in conducting comprehensive literature reviews by scanning vast amounts of academic papers and articles to extract relevant information and summarize key findings.

- » **Budget optimization.** AI algorithms can assist in optimizing budget allocation by analyzing historical data, project requirements, and funding constraints to suggest the most cost-effective allocation of resources.

- » **Predictive analytics.** AI can provide predictive analytics to forecast project outcomes, potential challenges, and the impact of various interventions, helping researchers make informed decisions and strengthen their proposals.

- » **Reviewer matching.** AI can help match grant proposals with appropriate reviewers based on their expertise and research interests, increasing the likelihood of receiving favorable evaluations.

- » **Risk assessment.** AI-powered risk assessment tools can identify potential risks associated with the proposed project, allowing researchers to address them proactively in their proposals.

- » **Compliance checking.** AI can assist in ensuring that the grant proposal complies with all relevant regulations, guidelines, and formatting requirements specified by the funding agency.

- » **Document management.** AI-driven document management systems can streamline the process of organizing, storing, and retrieving grant-related documents, improving collaboration and version control among team members.

- » **Grammar and style checking.** AI-driven grammar and style checking tools can help ensure that the proposal is free from grammatical errors, awkward phrasing, and inconsistencies.

AI SPOTLIGHT

Consider using these highly rated AI tools to assist your writing:

- » **ChatGPT:** https://chatgpt.com
- » **Grammarly:** https://www.grammarly.com
- » **Grantable:** https://www.grantable.co
- » **Grantboost.io:** https://grantboost.io
- » **Granter.ai:** https://granter.ai
- » **PitchPower:** https://pitchpower.ai

Remembering the Human Element — You!

To truly elevate your grant proposal into a masterpiece, you also need that special ingredient: Writer intelligence (WI). Use your WI to transform your grant proposal from ordinary to extraordinary — making you the undeniable recipient of that coveted grant funding. Find out more about using WI in Chapter 1.

Remembering the Human
Element — You!

Chapter **5**
Turning Prompts into Gold

Crafting effective AI prompts is like mining for gold. Just as you need the right tools, technique, and a bit of patience to strike it rich, crafting prompts requires preparation, precision, and focus. Well-structured prompts minimize confusion, reduce the need for follow-up questions, and enhance the user experience. So, dig in and learn to write prompts that get you the gold (or in your case the golden, coveted funding.)

SHERYL SAYS

A *prompt* is a specific input that's provided to an AI system to generate a desired output or response. In essence, it's AI-speak for posing a question. Throughout this book you'll see examples of prompts and the AI responses. They're in italics so you can recognize them easily.

This chapter shows you one of the key values of AI through writing prompts that not only get you the responses you need — but also make your chatbots think, "Wow, that's a question I can't resist answering!" Let's dive in and turn your curiosity into pure proposal-writing gold!

REMEMBER

You may need to re-write a prompt multiple times to get the best possible results, but those iterations are key to refining your own skills and understanding. Soon, you'll become a pro-prompter!

Using Prompts as Your Proposal-Writing GPS

To write an effective prompt, you need to blend clarity with creativity, ensuring your requests are precise yet open enough to inspire engaging and useful responses. While you can get by with a simple "misspeling" or omit a question mark at the end of a question, try to be as accurate as you can.

Here's how AI prompts can act as your GPS when writing a proposal:

>> **Enhancing creativity:** AI prompts can spark new ideas and directions for grant proposals. By suggesting alternative angles or methodologies, they can stimulate creative thinking among grant writers, leading to more innovative proposals.

>> **Improving efficiency:** Grant writing can be a time-consuming process, but AI prompts can help streamline it by generating relevant prompts, questions, or outlines tailored to the specific grant application. This can save valuable time for researchers and organizations, allowing them to focus on other aspects of the proposal.

>> **Providing quality assurance:** AI prompts can ensure that grant proposals address all necessary components and criteria. By prompting writers to consider various aspects such as project objectives, methodology, impact assessment, and budgeting, AI can help ensure that proposals are comprehensive and well rounded.

>> **Customizing:** Prompts can be customized based on the specific requirements of different grant applications whether it's a government grant, foundation grant, corporate grant, scholarship grant, research grant, emergency grant, or any others.

>> **Assisting with language enhancement:** AI prompts can assist in improving the language and clarity of grant proposals. By suggesting alternative phrasings, correcting grammar and spelling errors, and providing feedback on overall readability, AI can help grant writers communicate their ideas more effectively.

>> **Providing data analysis:** AI prompts can assist in data analysis and interpretation, which is often a crucial

component of grant proposals (especially in scientific research or social science projects). By suggesting analytical approaches or highlighting key insights from data, AI can strengthen the evidential basis of grant proposals.

>> **Supporting adaptability:** AI prompts can adapt to the evolving needs and priorities of grant writers. Whether it's refining the focus of the proposal, incorporating feedback from reviewers, or adjusting to changes in funding requirements, AI can provide ongoing support throughout the grant-writing process.

SHERYL
SAYS

It's okay to abandon the good manners you were taught about saying "please" and "thank you." AI doesn't require niceties; it's all about results. But I asked ChatGPT what it thought about this:

Prompt: *Should I say please and thank you when I ask you for something?*

AI's response: *I probably shouldn't tell you this, but feel free to throw etiquette out the window when dealing with me. I don't need "please" or "thank you" to get the job done. But, just remember, even though I'm a bunch of code, I still appreciate a little politeness. It's like giving a high-five to a robot — no matter how many times you do it, it never gets old!*

Crafting Your Proposal with Precise Prompts

WARNING

Not using precise prompts can lead to unclear or irrelevant responses, increased confusion, and the need for follow-up questions. It can also result in decreased accuracy, wasted resources, lower user satisfaction, missed opportunities, and ineffective communication.

SHERYL
SAYS

I opened this section with a negative to emphasize the importance of precision and potential pitfalls. Using the negative in your proposals to emphasize something to be avoided can sharpen the focus on the undesired outcome, making the warning more striking and memorable.

Table 5-1 shows examples of AI prompts that serve as good starting points, helping you to structure your proposals and address key components required for successful grant proposals.

Stephanie Diamond and Jeffrey Allan's *Writing AI Prompts For Dummies* (John Wiley & Sons, Inc., 2024) provides further help when crafting your perfect prompt.

TABLE 5-1 **Examples of AI Prompts for Specific Aspects of a Proposal**

Research Objectives and Hypotheses	*Please outline the primary research objectives of this project and any hypotheses it aims to test.*
	What specific research questions will address through this grant-funded project
	Describe how the research objectives align with the goals and priorities of the funding organization.
Methodology and Approach	*Detail the methodology to employ in the research, including data collection methods, sample size determination, and statistical analysis techniques.*
	How to ensure the validity and reliability of my research findings?
	Discuss any innovative or novel approaches to use in the research methodology.
Project Timeline and Milestones	*Provide a detailed timeline for the project, including key milestones and deliverables.*
	How to allocate resources and manage the project timeline to ensure timely completion.
	Identify any potential challenges or risks that may impact the project timeline and how to mitigate them.
Expected Impact and Significance	*Describe the potential impact of the research findings on the field and any broader societal implications.*
	Explain how the project contributes to advancing knowledge or addressing critical issues in [field].
	Discuss any plans for disseminating the research findings and engaging relevant stakeholders.

Budget Justification	*Provide a detailed budget breakdown for the project, including personnel, equipment, supplies, and other expenses.*
	Justify the requested budget by explaining how each expense contributes to the successful execution of the project.
	Discuss any potential sources of additional funding or in-kind contributions to support the project.
Evaluation and Assessment	*Outline plans for evaluating the success and impact of the project.*
	Describe the metrics or indicators to assess the effectiveness of my research outcomes.
	Discuss any plans for disseminating the evaluation findings and lessons learned.
Sustainability and Long-Term Impact	*Explain how to ensure the sustainability of the project beyond the grant period.*
	Discuss any plans for leveraging the project outcomes to secure future funding or partnerships.
	Describe how the project contributes to building capacity or infrastructure in my field or community.

Understanding the Capabilities and Limitations of AI Tools

WARNING

AI tools and chatbots have varying capabilities, so it's important to understand the strengths and limitations of the AI tool you're working with. For example, if the tool shines in generating creative narratives, you can design prompts that encourage storytelling to enhance documents such as grant proposals and bios.

On the other hand, if the AI tool is more adept at providing factual information, you can craft prompts that require the AI to research and present accurate data on a given topic. Check out Chapter 2 to see how chatbots responded differently to the same prompt.

The following sections highlight some of the key considerations to bear in mind to make your "conversations" efficient and productive.

Chatting away

Chatbots are quite adaptable and can handle both spoken and written prompts effortlessly. It's a bit like chatting with a colleague. You can ask for clarifications, request a follow-up, steer the conversation in a different direction, dive deeper into a topic, or even ask to change the tone or the response.

As shown in Figure 5-1, I asked ChatGPT a question and it gave me a response. Then I followed up with another question, and it responded to that too. I was happy with both answers, so I ended the chat — although I could have continued it if needed. Chatbots have lots of patience.

> **How can I have a conversation with you?**

You're already having one! Just type whatever you want to talk about or ask, and I'll do my best to respond. Whether you have questions, need advice, or just want to chat about something interesting, I'm here for it. What's on your mind today?

> **Why should I include graphics in an executive summary for a proposal?**

Including graphics in an executive summary for a proposal can be very effective for several reasons:

1. **Visual Appeal:** Graphics make your summary more engaging and visually appealing, which can help capture and hold the reader's attention.

2. **Clarity:** Complex data and concepts can often be communicated more clearly through visuals like charts, graphs, or infographics. This helps in making your key points more understandable at a glance.

3. **Quick Understanding:** Busy executives may not have time to read every detail. Graphics can quickly convey critical information and highlight the most important aspects of your proposal.

4. **Emphasis:** They help emphasize key data and conclusions, making it easier to see the impact and value of your proposal.

5. **Retention:** People often remember visual information better than text alone, so using graphics can help reinforce your message and ensure it sticks.

6. **Professionalism:** Well-designed graphics can enhance the overall professionalism of your proposal, showing that you've put thought and effort into presenting your ideas.

Just make sure the graphics are relevant, easy to understand, and not overly complex. They should support and enhance your narrative rather than overwhelm it.

FIGURE 5-1: A conversation with ChatGPT.

Asking for one single task at a time

Contrary to what we may think, humans aren't efficient multi-taskers. Our brains struggle with simultaneous task management, resulting in reduced productivity and more errors. AI shares a similar challenge with multitasking. It's more effective when you ask it one clear request at a time, allowing it to focus and deliver precise responses.

WARNING

Multiple requests in a single prompt can lead to confusion and hinder AI's ability to generate coherent responses, impacting the clarity and quality of the responses provided.

> **Prompt lacking clarity:** *I need information on the benefits of exercise, different types of exercises, how to create a workout routine, and the best diet plan to follow.*

> **Prompt with simplified single request:** *What are the benefits of exercise for overall health and well-being?*

Finding the right length

WARNING

Prompt writing is like Goldilocks's porridge; either too hot or too cold. Avoid the too-short prompt or the epic saga. Find that just-right middle ground. If not, you might find yourself getting spirited responses such as the ones below that I received on two separate occasions. I don't remember what my prompts were, but I do remember AI's two sassy responses:

> *Hey there, I'm all ears (figuratively speaking)! Could you toss a few more words my way so I can catch your drift? This prompt's a bit like a cryptic crossword without enough clues!*

> *Whoa, Shakespeare! Your verbosity is giving me digital indigestion. Mind simplifying things a tad?*

Providing specific guidelines and instructions

Provide specific guidelines such as word or page count, number of bullet points, formatting requirements, tone, or any specific elements or themes. Here are some examples of well-written prompts:

> *Write a persuasive 2-paragraph email to [name of client] who has shown an interest in purchasing [product] but can't commit because of budget constraints. List three purchase options.*

> *Write a series of 3 emails to follow up on a post-purchase to make customers know they're valued.*

> *Create an engaging two-paragraph introduction for an article on the pros and cons of [topic] starting with a pertinent analogy.*

> *Compose a 500-word blog on [topic].*

Asking open-ended questions

Asking AI open-ended questions unleashes creativity and imagination, allowing it to explore new ideas and concepts. This can lead to unexpected and fascinating outcomes, pushing the boundaries of what is known and venturing into new possibilities. Here are examples of open-ended prompts:

> *How can I strengthen the "impact" section of my grant proposal to clearly articulate the potential outcomes and benefits of the project to both the funding organization and the broader community?*

> *What are some innovative approaches to conducting literature reviews and citing relevant research in a grant proposal to demonstrate the project's feasibility and build a strong theoretical foundation?*

> *Could you provide insights on incorporating stakeholder engagement and collaboration strategies into a grant proposal to demonstrate project sustainability and enhance its competitiveness for funding?*

REMEMBER

Close-ended questions, such as those requiring "yes" or "no" answers, are effective when you need specific answers, concise responses, or feedback that can be easily analyzed. They provide a focused approach to communication and can help you get the information you need efficiently.

Using specific keywords or phrases

You can enhance AI's ability to generate more relevant ideas by incorporating specific keywords related to your industry, niche, or topic. (Learn more about this in Chapter 6.) As an example, if you're asking about dog breeds, include terms such as *breed, size, training*, and *temperament*. If you're talking about gardening, include keywords such as such as *organic, plants, soil*, or *fertilizer*.

Here are a couple of examples of prompts using some of these keywords:

> *Share tips on how to create a thriving organic garden. Make it conversational.*

> *Write an informative 500-word article about the best plants for beginners to grow in their garden. Provide essential care instructions.*

> *Which large dogs are obedient and easy to train?*

Indicating your desired tone

To indicate the tone, use descriptive words such as *friendly, enthusiastic, humorous, sympathetic, assertive, optimistic, cautious, professional, urgent, personalize, inspirational*, and so on. (Explore more about tone in Chapter 14.)

Here's an example of how to prompt a chatbot for the tone you want to project:

> **Prompt:** *Please personalize this: The organization aims to achieve its goals through various innovative methods.*

> **AI's response:** *Our organization is strongly committed to reaching our objectives using a wide range of creative techniques.*

Encouraging research

When writing AI prompts that encourage research, give clear and specific instructions while leaving room for the AI to explore and generate its own ideas. For example:

> *Explore the impact of climate change on marine ecosystems, considering both short-term and long-term effects.*

This prompt encourages the AI to research and provide a comprehensive analysis. Next, continue the conversation by asking AI to support its responses with evidence or examples. Remember to be patient, as this may be a reiterative process:

> *Provide three examples of scientific studies or research papers that support your analysis on [topic].*

Here are a few other examples of prompts that allow AI the freedom to do its own research:

> *Create an agenda for a meeting with my team. The meeting is about [insert meeting info]. Provide examples of what should be included in the agenda.*

> *Conduct market research on consumer preferences for eco-friendly products. Provide insights on current trends. You can then re-prompt for information on consumer buying behavior.*

> *Investigate sustainable energy solutions for reducing carbon emissions in urban areas.*

Calling Upon Writer Intelligence

WARNING

Even with AI's assistance, you still need sharp writer intelligence (WI) to perfect a grant proposal. While AI can do lots of wonderful things, it sometimes provides inaccurate or misleading information. A skilled proposal writer brings essential human elements — such as compelling stories and tailored content that aligns with the funder's goals — to ensure clarity, engagement, and persuasiveness. This human touch addresses potential concerns and enhances the proposal's impact.

Thus, despite AI's valuable contributions, human finesse remains crucial and irreplaceable.

Chapter **6**
Cracking the Keyword Code

In the feeding frenzy for grant funding, amidst the bustling eco-system of applications — where each word serves as a beacon guiding the way to financial enlightenment — there exists a hidden nirvana: Keywords. These linguistic gems are magical components embedded within your grant proposal. They have unparalleled potency in shaping the destiny of your proposal.

Consider for a moment that you're a job seeker working on your resume. You'd use specific keywords to highlight your skills and experiences, making sure they match what the job description is asking for. This way, both electronic scanners and human review-ers can see you're a great fit. Well, crafting a grant proposal is a lot like that. You need to use keywords that align with the funding agency's mission, goals, and evaluation criteria. These keywords help connect your project's objectives with what the funder is looking for.

SHERYL
SAYS

This chapter shows how AI can help to generate keywords that pop like fireworks on the Fourth of July — whether they're catch-ing the eye of human reviewers or their electronic counterparts. When it comes to getting noticed, the right keywords are your keys to the funding kingdom. Make those reviewers sit up and take notice!

Grasping the Importance of Keywords in the Review Process

In the realm of grants, where fortunes are won and lost on the strength of a well-crafted narrative, keywords wield immense power. They're not mere words, but strategic tools that captivate, persuade, and elevate your proposal above the noise of competition.

Keywords act as microscopic beacons under a scrutinizing lens, guiding grant proposals through the intricate terrain of evaluation. Whether scrutinized by a meticulous human reviewer or analyzed by an electronic scanner, keywords function as vital markers that ensure visibility and distinction in the following ways:

>> For human reviewers, keywords help experts quickly understand your project's relevance and impact, making it stand out and sparking interest.

>> For electronic scanners, keywords are crucial for passing automated checks. They help ensure your proposal is detected and considered by algorithms that search for specific terms.

REMEMBER

Here's how keywords play a pivotal role in conveying the essence of your project, including its purpose, problem statement, proposed solution, and anticipated impact, thereby increasing the proposal's chances of success:

>> **Highlighting relevance:** They indicate to reviewers that the proposal addresses key aspects of the grant's objectives and priorities. Using relevant keywords ensures the proposal is aligned with the funding agency's goals.

>> **Enhancing searchability:** Keywords help funding agencies and reviewers quickly find proposals that match specific criteria or focus areas. This improves the visibility and accessibility of the proposal among potentially hundreds of submissions.

>> **Clarifying focus and impact:** Well-chosen keywords succinctly communicate the proposal's main themes, objectives, and expected outcomes. They provide clarity on what the project aims to achieve and how it contributes to broader goals.

>> **Demonstrating expertise:** Using appropriate keywords demonstrates the proposer's understanding of the subject matter and their ability to articulate its importance within the context of the grant's purpose. This reinforces credibility and expertise.

>> **Facilitating evaluation:** Reviewers often use keywords as initial filters or criteria to assess the relevance and potential impact of a proposal. Clear and compelling keywords can therefore influence the initial impression and subsequent evaluation of the proposal.

WARNING

Neglecting to include strategic keywords in your grant proposal can significantly jeopardize its chances of success. Without these critical markers, your proposal may easily get lost in the flood of submissions, overlooked by both human reviewers and electronic scanners.

Adding the Value of AI

AI SPOTLIGHT

AI can be a powerful tool for identifying keywords in grant proposals by analyzing large amounts of text data efficiently. Here's a breakdown of how AI can help identify keywords for a grant proposal:

>> **Seeing what stands out:** Highlighting words that are unique or different compared to other proposals. These standout words can be important for making the proposal stand out.

>> **Adapting to different audiences:** Adjusting the choice of words based on who will be reading the proposal. It can suggest words that are more likely to resonate with specific reviewers or funding agencies.

>> **Understanding patterns:** Studying many grant proposals to find common words and phrases that successful proposals often use. This helps it figure out which keywords are important for a particular type of grant.

>> **Extracting important words:** Picking out keywords from a grant proposal or related documents. These words usually describe the project's goals, methods, and expected results.

>> **Improving over time:** Suggesting keywords because it learns from feedback. As researchers and reviewers use it more, it learns which suggestions work best and adjusts its recommendations.

>> **Learning from feedback:** Learning from examples and feedback on past proposals to understand which words were effective in getting grants approved. It uses this knowledge to suggest similar words for new proposals.

>> **Checking for accuracy:** Ensuring that the words chosen are accurate and relevant to the topic of the grant proposal. It can flag words that might not fit well or suggest better alternatives.

In Figure 6-1 you see the response to the following prompt:

Identify keywords for a grant proposal on cancer research.

I continued the conversation and asked AI the following:

Expand with 10 words as they relate specifically to clinical trials.

You see the response in Figure 6-2.

1. Oncology

2. Tumor biology

3. Immunotherapy

4. Precision medicine

5. Biomarkers

6. Chemotherapy resistance

7. Metastasis

8. Genomic instability

9. Targeted therapy

10. Clinical trials

FIGURE 6-1: Using AI to identify cancer research keywords.

1. Randomized controlled trials (RCTs)

2. Phase I/II/III trials

3. Patient recruitment

4. Informed consent

5. Adverse events (AEs)

6. Protocol adherence

7. Endpoint assessment

8. Data monitoring committee (DMC)

9. Pharmacokinetics (PK) and pharmacodynamics (PD)

10. Regulatory compliance

FIGURE 6-2: Expanding the keyword search to focus on clinical trials.

AI SPOTLIGHT

Here are a few AI tools that can help you identify keywords:

>> **Ahrefs (https://ahrefs.com):** Offers detailed keyword analysis and suggestions.

>> **SEMrush (https://www.semrush.com):** Provides keyword research and competitive analysis.

>> **SpyFu (https://www.spyfu.com):** Focuses on competitor analysis, showing which keywords your competitors are ranking for and their paid search strategies. It's helpful for understanding competitive landscapes.

UNEARTHING SIGNIFICANT KEYWORDS

Here are some hints to finding just the right linguistic gems in addition to using AI:

- **Reviewing grant guidelines:** Look for words or phrases that are repeated frequently or emphasized, as these are likely key priorities for the funder and will be identified by the reviewers.

- **Identifying your target audience:** What are their needs, interests, and priorities? What are their goals, missions, and values?

(continued)

(continued)

What are the key terms and concepts that they use to describe their areas of focus and funding criteria? This information may be available on the website or in the Request for Proposal (RFP; see Chapter 11).

- **Using online tools and resources:** Learn what keywords and phrases are popular and relevant in the field and topic. Tap into search engines, databases, journals, websites, blogs, social media, and other sources to see what terms and phrases are frequently used and searched for by your peers and competitors.

- **Consulting experts:** Reach out to experts in your field for their insights on important keywords or terminology relevant to your proposal. This may be co-workers, influencers, journalists, or other recognized experts. They may provide valuable suggestions based on their experience and knowledge.

Avoiding Keyword Overload

To ensure your grant proposal maintains its authenticity and avoids the pitfall of keyword overload, use AI to help identify synonyms or related terms. This not only prevents redundancy but also demonstrates a richer vocabulary and a deeper understanding of the topic.

Strive for a delicate balance between natural language flow and forced insertions. That means seamlessly weaving them into your narrative. Let the keywords serve as subtle signposts that enhance the clarity and coherence of your ideas, rather than imposing themselves as conspicuous distractions. Prioritize clarity, coherence, and sincerity in your writing, allowing the essence of your research vision to shine through organically.

REMEMBER

A well-crafted proposal resonates not just for its keywords, but for the depth of its insight and the passion behind its pursuit.

IN THIS CHAPTER

» Using AI as your virtual writing assistant

» Getting AI to help with keywords

» Polishing your draft with writer intelligence

» Checking carefully before submitting your proposal

Chapter **7**
Defeating Writer's Block

S am sat at his desk in the bustling office of a nonprofit organization. He was surrounded by stacks of papers and a looming deadline for a crucial grant proposal he needed to write for funding mental health services in a high school. These services would include accessible support programs, counseling, therapy, and education. The clock ticked mercilessly as Sam stared at the blank screen at a loss for words and ideas. *Writer's block* (that feeling when you need to write but the words just don't come) had hit him hard, like a sudden traffic jam on a familiar route. Each attempt to articulate his organization's mission seemed to hit a dead end, leaving him frustrated and uncertain.

Just when he felt like he was drowning in the storm of his own thoughts, Sam remembered a conversation he had with a few colleagues about using AI to streamline the drafting process. With a glimmer of hope, he decided to try ChatGPT. (As you read this book, you'll find references to popular chatbots used for specific purposes; you'll also find many of the popular general-purpose chatbots listed in Chapter 1.) ChatGPT began to organize his ideas like a reliable GPS system guiding him through the chaotic traffic of his thought. It was as if Sam had a co-pilot navigating, showing him ways to bypass traffic by using alternate routes.

With each suggestion from the chatbot, Sam felt his creativity reignite, much like the revitalizing effect of his morning espresso. It rejuvenated his energy and motivation, giving him the boost he needed to overcome writer's block and draft his grant proposal.

As he reviewed the draft, Sam couldn't help but feel grateful for the assistance of ChatGPT in navigating through the storm of grant writing, turning what felt like an insurmountable challenge into a manageable journey towards success.

SHERYL SAYS

If you've ever found yourself staring at a blank screen, wondering where to begin, fear not! This chapter shows you how AI can be your secret weapon to busting through writer's block and kicking off your writing journey with a bang. With the help of AI you can turn that blank page into a canvas of endless possibilities!

Writing a Draft with AI as Your Virtual Assistant

AI SPOTLIGHT

Using AI chatbots such as ChatGPT (`https://chatgpt.com`), Copilot (`https://copilot.microsoft.com`), HubSpot (`https://www.hubspot.com`), and others you can experience the marvel of AI technology mixed with your own writer intelligence (WI) to get your draft started and eliminate the dreaded writer's block.

Using AI for this purpose is like bouncing ideas off a specialist to get unstuck. Let's revisit Sam's writer's block to work through an example of this. The following is the prompt Sam created and typed into ChatGPT:

> *Create a grant proposal for mental health services in the high school to include accessible support programs, counseling, therapy, and education. Also include a reasonable budget.*

Figures 7-1 and 7-2 show the two-page draft that ChatGPT generated. Remember that AI isn't perfect . . . you'll notice that the numbers were kind of wonky. But no worries, Sam made the corrections afterwards.

Grant Proposal: Enhancing Mental Health Services in High Schools

Introduction: Mental health issues among high school students are a growing concern with significant implications for academic performance, social functioning, and overall well-being. Research indicates that early intervention and access to mental health services can mitigate these challenges and promote positive outcomes. This grant proposal aims to enhance mental health services in our high school through the implementation of accessible support programs, counseling, therapy, and education initiatives.

Objectives:

5. To establish a comprehensive mental health support system within the high school to address the diverse needs of students.
6. To provide timely and accessible counseling and therapy services to students experiencing mental health challenges.
7. To promote mental health awareness and education among students, teachers, and parents to reduce stigma and facilitate early intervention.
8. To create a supportive and inclusive school environment that prioritizes the mental well-being of all students.

Program Components:

6. **Counseling and Therapy Services:** Employ licensed counselors and therapists to provide individual and group counseling sessions for students. These sessions will address a range of mental health concerns including anxiety, depression, stress management, and interpersonal relationships.
7. **Peer Support Programs:** Implement peer support programs where trained student mentors offer support, guidance, and empathy to their peers experiencing mental health difficulties. These programs foster a sense of community and reduce the sense of isolation often felt by students struggling with mental health issues.
8. **Parent Education Workshops:** Organize workshops and seminars for parents to increase their understanding of adolescent mental health issues, warning signs, and available resources. Empowering parents with knowledge and skills will enable them to support their children effectively.
9. **Teacher Training and Support:** Provide training sessions for teachers and staff members to recognize signs of distress in students and learn appropriate strategies for offering support. Additionally, establish a system for teachers to refer students to the counseling and therapy services as needed.
10. **Mental Health Education Curriculum:** Integrate mental health education into the existing curriculum to promote understanding, resilience, and self-care among students. Topics may include stress management techniques, coping strategies, and promoting positive mental health habits.

FIGURE 7-1: First page of the draft generated by AI before Sam corrected the numbering.

Budget:

5. Personnel:
   - Licensed Counselors and Therapists: $100,000/year (2 full-time positions)
   - Peer Support Program Coordinator: $30,000/year (part-time)
   - Training and Development for Staff: $10,000/year
6. Program Implementation:
   - Materials for Workshops and Education Programs: $5,000/year
   - Peer Support Program Resources: $3,000/year
   - Curriculum Development for Mental Health Education: $7,000/year
7. Facilities and Equipment:
   - Counseling Room Renovation and Furnishing: $15,000 (one-time)
   - Technology and Software for Teletherapy Services: $8,000/year
8. Outreach and Awareness:
   - Marketing and Promotion of Services: $5,000/year
   - Parent Education Workshop Expenses: $2,000/year

Total Budget: $185,000/year

Evaluation: Regular evaluation and assessment of the program will be conducted to measure its effectiveness and identify areas for improvement. Metrics such as student attendance, academic performance, self-reported mental health outcomes, and satisfaction surveys will be utilized to gauge the impact of the program on the overall well-being of students.

Conclusion: Investing in the mental health of high school students is crucial for their academic success, personal development, and long-term well-being. By implementing comprehensive mental health services, counseling, therapy, and education initiatives, we can create a supportive and nurturing environment where all students can thrive. This grant proposal seeks to secure funding to realize this vision and make a positive difference in the lives of our students.

FIGURE 7-2: Second page of the draft generated by AI before Sam corrected the numbering.

Sam then asked ChatGPT to take it to the next level by creating a table from the budgeted items. Figure 7-3 shows the results.

AI SPOTLIGHT

Here are some popular tools for drafting your proposal. While Chapter 1 covers additional tools specifically for grant writing, these are more broadly applicable. However, all will do the job!

>> **Canva's Magic Write:** https://www.canva.com/magic-write

- ≫ **Copy.ai:** https://www.copy.ai
- ≫ **Delilah:** https://www.delilah.ai
- ≫ **Grammarly:** https://app.grammarly.com
- ≫ **Hix.ai:** https://hix.ai
- ≫ **HyperWrite:** https://www.hyperwriteai.com
- ≫ **Jasper:** https://www.jasper.ai
- ≫ **Rytr:** https://rytr.me

Budget Item	Annual Cost	One-time Cost
Personnel:		
- Licensed Counselors and Therapists	$100,000	
- Peer Support Program Coordinator	$30,000	
- Training and Development for Staff	$10,000	
Program Implementation:		
- Materials for Workshops and Education Programs	$5,000	
- Peer Support Program Resources	$3,000	
- Curriculum Development for Mental Health Education	$7,000	
Facilities and Equipment:		
- Counseling Room Renovation and Furnishing		$15,000
- Technology and Software for Teletherapy Services	$8,000	
Outreach and Awareness:		
- Marketing and Promotion of Services	$5,000	
- Parent Education Workshop Expenses	$2,000	

Total Annual Budget: $170,000
Total One-time Cost: $15,000

FIGURE 7-3: Table created by AI from raw numbers.

Each tool is slightly different, but there are certain fields you'll be asked to fill in when asking for a little bit of AI-generated help:

- ≫ **Type of document:** Email, article, summary, press release, and so forth.
- ≫ **Key points:** The main points you want addressed.
- ≫ **Tone:** Formal, informal, joyful, sincere, sad, and so on.
- ≫ **Length:** Number of words or pages.

Sleuthing the Right Keywords with AI

Sam then asked ChatGPT to provide the keywords as he moved the proposal beyond the initial draft stage. (Learn more about keywords in Chapter 6.) Figure 7-4 shows what the chatbot produced.

1. **Mental Health Services:** Clearly state the focus of the program.

2. **High School:** Specify the target population.

3. **Prevention:** Emphasize the proactive nature of the program.

4. **Early Intervention:** Highlight the importance of addressing mental health issues early.

5. **Well-being:** Stress the goal of promoting overall mental well-being.

6. **Crisis Management:** Indicate readiness to address urgent mental health needs.

7. **Counseling:** Mention the availability of professional counseling services.

8. **Peer Support:** Include any peer support programs that may be part of the initiative.

9. **Education and Awareness:** Signal efforts to educate students and staff about mental health.

10. **Stigma Reduction:** If applicable, discuss strategies for reducing the stigma around mental health.

11. **Community Partnerships:** Highlight collaborations with local mental health organizations or professionals.

12. **Data-Driven:** Indicate that the program's effectiveness will be measured using data.

13. **Evidence-Based Practices:** Mention any interventions or approaches that are evidence-based.

14. **Sustainability:** Discuss plans for the program's long-term sustainability.

15. **Equity and Access:** Emphasize the importance of providing equitable access to mental health services for all students.   ↓

FIGURE 7-4: Finding the right keywords with the help of AI.

REPURPOSING EXISTING CONTENT

Repurposing existing content in the context of proposals means strategically using previously created material to enhance the quality and efficiency of your proposal-writing process. By repurposing content from past proposals, presentations, case studies, marketing materials, or proposals that were previously successful, you can save valuable time and resources while maintaining consistency in messaging and branding. This allows you to focus more on crafting compelling narratives and strategic insights tailored to specific client needs, thereby increasing productivity and improving the overall impact of your proposals.

AI tools can scan and analyze previous materials to identify sections that are relevant to your current proposal. However, it's essential to ensure that all reused content is relevant, updated as necessary, and properly credited to maintain integrity and transparency.

Polishing the Draft by Pairing WI and AI

Enough about Sam . . . Let's level up from creating your own draft to crafting your polished proposal that not only captures your vision but dazzles the grant reviewer with its clarity and persuasiveness.

Buffing it up with WI

Once AI has helped you create a basic draft, you need to add WI's human touch. (Tap into why this is so important by reading Chapter 1).

REMEMBER

As a proposal writer, there are some crucial considerations that demand your attention — areas where AI can't offer insight or judgment:

>> **Will the cover letter wow the reviewer?** This is the first impression that will determine whether they discard your proposal or continue reading. (Chapter 8 is chock-full of tips.)

>> **Do the headlines give key information at a glance?** If headlines and subheads don't jump out with key information, revise them. (Chapter 3 fills you in on writing pop-out headlines.)

>> **Is there a strong problem statement?** Without a strong problem statement that clearly defines the issue and its significance, your proposal will lack focus, and reviewers may have difficulty seeing the relevance of your project. (Learn more about creating a problem statement in Chapter 4.)

>> **Did I use paragraphs appropriately?** Limit paragraphs to eight lines of text. If paragraphs are too long, people may not read them. If they're too short, your message may seem disjointed.

>> **Are keywords sprinkled throughout?** This will enhance the proposal's visibility and relevance, ensuring it aligns with search criteria and increases the likelihood of attracting attention from targeted reviewers or evaluators. (Chapter 6 gives details on how AI can help you find keywords.)

>> **Is the tone correct?** The language and style should align with the values and expectations of the funding organization while maintaining clarity and professionalism. (Learn about using the proper tone in Chapter 14.)

>> **Did I give too much or too little information?** Provide the needed information to ensure clarity, relevance, and optimal engagement without overwhelming or underwhelming the reviewers.

>> **Are there adequate transitions?** Used sparingly, transitions such as *moreover, however*, and *therefore* between ideas can help the reviewer keep track of how your arguments are related to one another.

>> **Did I include critical stories?** Remember that stories forge human connections by engaging emotions and creating empathy, thereby swaying the grantor to allocate the funds you request. (Creating winning stories is detailed in Chapter 3.)

>> **Did I add testimonials?** These serve as social proof by validating the credibility and effectiveness of your proposed solution through real-world experiences and feedback from satisfied stakeholders or users.

Proofreading and editing with AI

Harness the power of AI to meticulously proofread and edit every section of your proposal, from the captivating front matter that hooks the reviewer to the detailed back matter that adds depth and credibility.

AI tools excel in catching grammar and punctuation errors, ensuring consistency in style and formatting, and even offering suggestions for clearer phrasing and more impactful language. Tools include Grammarly (https://app.grammarly.com), QuillBot (https://quillbot.com/online-proofreader), and Trinka (https://www.trinka.ai/free-proofreading-tools). However, chatbots also proofread and edit their own output.

Readying Your Proposal for Submission

Readying your proposal for submission is like baking a cake. You know it's ready when all the ingredients have been carefully measured and mixed, the batter is smooth and consistent, and it's been baked to perfection. Just as a cake needs to be delicious, well decorated, and meet the expectations of those who will enjoy it, a proposal needs to be polished, persuasive, and meet all the required guidelines.

If you've used AI as an assistant to get you this far, humans alone are critical at this point. They bring contextual understanding, nuanced judgment, and creativity that AI can't provide. Only humans can ensure that the final output aligns with specific goals, addresses subtleties, and resonates effectively with the reviewers.

Never power up your computer and shut down your brain — let AI keep your mind in gear rather than doing the driving.

3
Making a Great
First Impression

Discover the power of the cover letter and let AI turn your first impressions into funding fireworks.

Get your grant proposal to shine with the help of an AI-crafted, show-stopping title page that steals the spotlight.

Impress decision makers by using AI to whip up an executive summary that packs a punch and wins them over in a flash.

Chapter **8**

Harnessing the Influence of the Cover Letter

A compelling cover letter in a grant proposal is like crafting the perfect dish for a prestigious culinary competition. Just as each ingredient must blend to create an outstanding flavor, your cover letter must blend seamlessly to captivate the senses of the funding organization. It's not merely about making a good initial impression but about crafting a culinary master-piece that will leave a lasting taste on the palate of the potential funder.

Much like how a chef carefully selects the freshest ingredients, you must choose your words with precision, ensuring they resonate with the values and goals of the funding organization while authentically representing your mission and vision. And just as a skilled chef infuses their dish with passion and creativity, infuse your cover letter with the essence of your project's purpose and potential impact.

So, whether you're crafting a culinary masterpiece or a cover letter, remember the significance is not just the first impression, but the *right* first impression. Just as a well-prepared dish can win over the toughest of food critics, a well-crafted cover letter can secure the support needed to turn your vision into reality.

REMEMBER

Despite its name, a cover letter isn't always a letter in the traditional sense. It can also be an email or electronic letter accompanying an online proposal submission.

SHERYL
SAYS

This chapter shows how — with AI as your virtual assistant — your cover letter can swoop in, set the stage with charm and wit, and hook your reviewer from the start. Discover its secret powers. It's not just a formality but your proposal's unforgettable first impression.

Prioritizing the Reader's Perspective

SHERYL
SAYS

To illustrate the importance of the cover letter and how it can prioritize the reader's perspective, take a look at Figure 8-1, which showcases a letter received by one of my clients, an architectural firm. They had issued a Request for Proposal (RFP; find out more about these in Chapter 11), for a multi-million-dollar contract. The cover letter squelched any chances of this submitter getting the contract. As a matter of fact, my client never even read the proposal. Here's why: The sender mentioned themselves a staggering 28 times, while mentioning my client a mere three times. Then my client proudly announced, "And you know what I did? I responded to them with the following: 28 to 3 — you lose!"

REMEMBER

This scenario drives home the point of making the reader your priority. Use *you, your, we,* and *our* as much as you can to bring the reader (in this case funder) into focus.

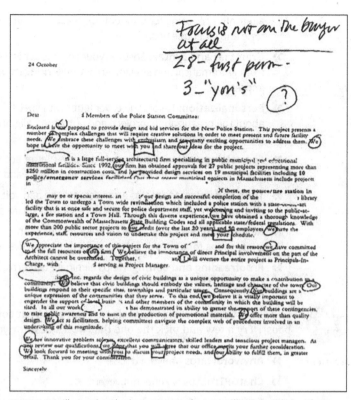

FIGURE 8-1: Illustrating the importance of a compelling cover letter that's not all about you.

Garnering AI's Assistance

AI
SPOTLIGHT

From spicing up your language to finely tailoring every word you write, here's how AI can sprinkle some magic over your cover letter:

- » **Keyword optimization:** Identifies and incorporates effective keywords and phrases into your cover letter to boost its relevance and visibility, particularly as AI-generated reviewers become more common. (See Chapter 6 for details.)

- » **Content suggestions:** Analyzes successful proposals and cover letters to offer insights and suggestions for including relevant points based on your project's goals and impact.

- » **Language enhancement:** Refines the clarity, coherence, and professionalism of your cover letter, suggesting alternative phrasing for greater impact. (See Chapter 14 for tone and language tips.)

>> **Grammar and syntax:** Ensures your cover letter is free from grammatical and spelling errors, enhancing its overall impression.

>> **Personalization:** Tailors the cover letter with specific details about the organization, project, and outcomes, aligning with grant requirements.

>> **Formatting assistance:** Formats the cover letter according to grant guidelines, including spacing, font styles, and layout.

>> **Tone and voice:** Maintains a consistent tone and voice, aligning with your organization's values and objectives.

>> **Review and feedback:** Offers instant feedback and suggestions for improving the cover letter's effectiveness.

>> **Proofreading and editing:** Helps eliminate text errors that could lead to rejection.

Check out these awesome AI tools that can give your cover letter a boost! Try a few and pick the one that works best for you:

>> **Anyword:** https://anyword.com

>> **ChatGPT:** https://chatgpt.com

>> **Copy.ai:** https://www.copy.ai

>> **Grammarly:** https://www.grammarly.com

>> **Jasper:** https://www.jasper.ai

>> **Rytr:** https://rytr.me

>> **Writesonic:** https://writesonic.com

As valuable as AI tools may be, remember that writer intelligence (WI) is critical. AI should be used as a complement to your creativity and critical thinking, rather than a replacement.

Including the "Write" Stuff

Whether you're sending your proposal online, via email, or by hard copy, your cover letter should look something like the one you see in Figure 8-2. And your cover letter should be prepared on a letterhead sheet (not shown in the figure).

[Date]

Grantor's Name and Title
Organization Institution
Street Address
City, State, Zip Code

Dear [Specific name]:

Please join us in our noble cause to provide tiny homes for disabled veterans, a gesture that honors those courageous Americans who fearlessly defended the very essence of our nation's values and freedoms. Having selflessly served this beautiful country, they deserve nothing short of our utmost respect and unwavering support.

It's with a fervent commitment to their well-being that I send this proposal, believing wholeheartedly in the transformative power of tiny home living as a beacon of hope and comfort for those who have sacrificed so much Let's join forces to turn this compassionate vision into a tangible reality, ensuring our veterans receive the dignity and assistance they rightfully deserve.

Some of the unique challenges faced by disabled veterans in finding accessible and affordable housing solutions can be helped with a grant of $250,000. That will enable hundreds of veterans with not only a safe and supportive environment but also a sense of community and belonging. Our proposed initiatives include:

- **Housing assistance:** Providing financial support for veterans to acquire or build their own tiny homes within designated communities.
- **Accessibility enhancements:** Ensuring that tiny homes are designed and equipped to meet the specific needs of disabled veterans, including wheelchair accessibility and adaptive features.
- **Supportive services:** Offering comprehensive support services, such as counseling, vocational training, and social activities, to promote veterans' overall well-being and integration into the community.
- **Sustainable development:** Implementing eco-friendly practices and promoting sustainable living principles within tiny home communities to minimize environmental impact and foster a sense of stewardship among residents.

By investing in this initiative, we can honor the sacrifices made by our nation's veterans and create a blueprint for innovative solutions to address the housing crisis facing this population. Let's build a brighter future for disabled veterans and pave the way for inclusive and resilient communities nationwide.

Thank you for considering this proposal.

Most sincerely,

Name, Title

Our true American heroes deserve the best our country has to offer. Together we can help them rebuild their lives with dignity.

FIGURE 8-2: This cover letter includes all of the key elements.

The following sections guide you through the different elements of a well-written cover letter, showing you what to include.

Capturing hearts and opening wallets

The cover letter sets the stage for your grant request and can significantly influence the funder's perception of your organization and project. Here are my top tips for what to include in an effective cover letter:

>> **Introduction:** This provides an overview of who you are, what you do, and why you're seeking funding. This helps funders quickly understand the context of your proposal before delving into the details.

>> **Personalization:** Personalize your proposal for the specific funder you're targeting. You can tailor your message to address the funder's interests, goals, and priorities, demonstrating that you've done your research and understand their needs. Also, if you've had previous (favorable) contact with the grant provider, mention that.

Personalized communication can make a significant difference in how your grant proposal is received. Taking the time to address it to the right person says more than what's written. It demonstrates your attention to detail and your genuine interest in partnering for the grant opportunity.

>> **Relationship building:** Start building a relationship with the funder. Express your appreciation for their work, demonstrate your enthusiasm for the opportunity to collaborate, and convey your commitment to achieving mutual goals.

>> **Clarity and conciseness:** The text must be clear, concise, and to the point. It should effectively communicate the purpose of your proposal, the impact you aim to achieve, and why the funder should consider supporting your project. This clarity helps ensure that your proposal gets the attention it deserves.

>> **Call to action (CTA):** Ending with a CTA, saying exactly what you expect the funder to do, invites them to review your attached proposal or inviting further discussion. This encourages the funder to take the next step and engage with your proposal, increasing the likelihood of a positive response. The CTA can be offering to clarify any issues, requesting a meeting, or thanking them for considering partnering with you.

Grabbing attention with a captivating opening paragraph

Start your letter with something that will captivate attention: A bold question. A shocking statistic. A statement. A story of a specific person or situation that your project has helped. This gives the reader a glimpse into your world and reminds them why your mission is important. Appeal to their hearts by giving specific details which tie directly into the project's goals and the funder's interests.

Here's an example of how AI can help to captivate a funder:

> **Prompt:** *In a few sentences tell about how hundreds of children in our community go to bed hungry and what we can do together to change that. Use a tone that tugs at heartstrings.*

> **AI's response:** *Every day, hundreds of children in our own community go to bed hungry. Together we can provide nutritious meals to these vulnerable children and give them a chance for a brighter future. Imagine the joy in a child's eyes as they receive a warm meal, knowing that someone cares enough to make a difference in their lives.*

Using a proper salutation and closing

Be aware of professional boundaries. The salutations and closing should align with the purpose and tone of your letter, your relationship and familiarity with the recipient, the culture and expectations of the recipient, and the consistency and clarity of your message. By providing the correct tone, you're setting a formal or informal tone that will carry through your letter. (Find out more about tone in Chapter 14.)

Saying hello

Salutations are important because they set the mood and determine the attitude your reviewer should adopt when responding. It's like saying hello to someone who walks into a room or calls you on the phone.

Always start with *Dear [Name]* (even though the person probably isn't dear to you). If you're writing to someone you don't know well (which is probably the case with proposals), use *Dear Mr., Mrs., Ms.,* or *Dr.* and the last name, followed by a colon. If you call the person by their first name (which is rare in the case of proposals), end with a comma. If you're unsure of the person's gender, use the first and last name followed by a colon:

» **Formal:** *Dear Mr. Gentry:*

» **Informal:** *Dear Leslie,*

» **Unsure of gender:** *Dear Pat Smith:*

Never use generic salutations such as *To Whom it May Concern* or *Dear Sir or Madam.* They're cold and impersonal. When you personalize your letter by addressing it to a specific person, you increase the chances of your letter being read and taken seriously.

Bidding adieu

A complimentary closing ends the letter with a professional touch. It demonstrates that you're adhering to standard communication etiquette. Just as you wouldn't ignore a hello when entering a room or calling on the phone, you wouldn't end a conversation without a proper goodbye:

» **Formal:** *Respectfully, Sincerely, Most sincerely.*

» **Informal:** *Best regards, Cordially, With appreciation.*

The closing doesn't end there. It's the beginning of a block of information that has the name of the sender and the person's title that can be expressed in either of the following ways. Be sure to leave enough room for the signature.

Sincerely yours,   *Sincerely yours,*

Douniya Crawford, Manager   *Douniya Crawford, Manager*

Ending with a postscript

Did you know that a postscript may be the most often read part of the cover letter? It stands apart from the body and grabs the recipient's eye. Use the postscript to emphasize collaboration and the importance of the recipient's involvement in the project:

In Figure 8-2, I prompted ChatGPT as follows: *Write a postscript to end the letter dramatically.* See how the chatbot nailed it!

REMEMBER

You don't need to add a "P.S." notation; the postscript is obvious without it. And if you handwrite it or use a script font, it will be even more powerful.

IN THIS CHAPTER

» Discovering the value of an impactful title

» Turning to AI for title-page assistance

» Using visuals to your advantage

» Including the right information

» Checking content carefully

Chapter 9

Amplifying the Impact of the Title Page

Assessing the title page of your proposal is like judging a book by its cover. We all do it! Although not heavy on content, the title page carries lots of weight. It's the first "hello" reviewers get after your cover letter — often just a quick glance. But it sets the tone for the rest of the proposal. A tidy, error-free title page isn't just eye candy; it's a billboard for your professionalism. It can sway what reviewers think of your proposal even before they dive into the meaty bits, just like the cover of a book.

SHERYL SAYS

This chapter demonstrates how seemingly small details can pack a punch and make the title page of your proposal stand out — for the right reasons. Get ready to jazz up your proposal using AI because your killer title and a snazzy title page are about to take center stage!

Knowing the Value of a Well-Chosen Title

Consider the transformative journey of two iconic literary works: *Men Are From Mars, Women Are From Venus* and the *Chicken Soup* series. Originally, these titles were but mere whispers in the vast cacophony of publishing, carrying the weight of their content but lacking the magnetic pull that would launch them into the stratosphere of success.

John Gray's seminal work on relationships was originally titled *Men, Women and Relationships*. Yet, it was the celestial imagery and gendered metaphor of *Men Are From Mars, Women Are From Venus* (HarperCollins, 1992) that catapulted Gray's book into the collective consciousness, resonating with readers worldwide and sparking a cultural phenomenon.

Similarly, the *Chicken Soup* series, compiled by Jack Canfield and Mark Victor Hansen, began its journey with a less-than-remarkable title: *Heartwarming Stories for the Soul*. While descriptive, it lacked the zing needed to capture the imagination of readers. It wasn't until the evocative simplicity of *Chicken Soup for the Soul* (Simon & Schuster, 1992) graced the covers that the series took flight, becoming a staple on bookshelves and inspiring countless readers with its nourishing tales of hope and resilience.

These are just two poignant reminders of the transformative power of a well-chosen title, and that the nuances of language, imagery, and emotion can turn a mundane title into a grant-proposal masterpiece.

JOURNEYING BACK IN TIME

SHERYL SAYS

As I was writing this chapter, I couldn't help but journey back to my early days as a workshop facilitator. I had put together a workshop titled, "Business and Technical Writing for Excellence." This fell flatter than a deflated balloon. Shortly thereafter I attended a professional networking event, where minds mingled and creativity crackled in the air. We set aside time to brainstorm, to muse and ponder perfect monikers. Lo and behold, amidst the whirlwind of ideas, a stroke of brilliance came to me.

There it was, gleaming like a beacon of linguistic delight: "Write It So They'll Read It™." Suddenly, a title that was once flat was transformed into something vibrant and dynamic, akin to a fully inflated balloon floating high in the sky. It was bursting with potential, excitement, and possibilities, and — with this energized title — the workshop soared (and continues to soar) to new heights. Oh, the power of a well-crafted title!

AI wasn't around then. But just for fun, I recently brainstormed with my favorite chatbot and asked it to generate titles for a workshop on business and technical writing:

Prompt: *Write 6 titles for a workshop on business writing and technical writing. Make them engaging.*

AI's response:

- *Write to Thrive: Bridging Business and Tech*
- *Crafting Clarity: The Art of Business Communication*
- *Wordsmiths Unite: Mastering Business & Technical Writing*
- *Ink & Algorithms: Navigating the Intersection of Business and Tech Writing*
- *The Power Pen: Transforming Ideas into Effective Business Communications*
- *From Code to Comprehension: Elevating Business Communication in the Tech Age*

They're good, but my title is where the magic happens and I'm sticking with it!

Getting Title-Page Help from AI

An informative title can summarize the entire proposal in one phrase. It's a big job, and a vital one. AI can streamline the process of title selection by offering a diverse range of options, refining language, and considering the needs and preferences of the intended audience. Here are some of the benefits of using AI to come up with a title:

>> **Generating options:** AI can quickly generate numerous title options based on the provided topic or keywords. This saves time and provides a pool of choices to consider using as a starting point.

>> **Offering variety and creativity:** AI can produce titles that encompass different angles, themes, or aspects of the proposal. It can offer a range of creative ideas that might not have been initially considered. (Dive into Chapter 1 to learn more about what chatbots are available. Try a few because they will each give different results.)

>> **Polishing language:** AI can refine titles by ensuring they're grammatically correct, concise, and engaging. It can suggest improvements to make the titles more appealing and professional.

>> **Considering the audience:** AI can analyze the target audience and tailor titles accordingly. It can adjust language, tone, and style to resonate with the specific audience, whether it's academic reviewers, funding organizations, or the general public. (Chapter 4 is your gateway to knowing all you can about your learners.)

>> **Incorporating feedback:** If the AI you're using has access to feedback or data on previously successful grant proposals, it can use this information to generate titles that align with patterns of success.

>> **Using keyword optimization:** AI can help ensure that titles contain relevant keywords or phrases that are likely to catch the attention of reviewers or funding bodies. This can improve the visibility and relevance of the proposal, especially for those that are reviewed online. (See Chapter 6 for tidbits on finding just the right keywords.)

In Figures 9-1 and 9-2 you see two examples of title suggestions generated by AI. Here are the prompts that generated those responses:

> **Prompt for Figure 9-1:** *Give me 5 grant proposal titles for an after-school program for elementary students. Make it appeal to grant reviewers.*

> **Prompt for Figure 9-2:** *List 5 titles for a research project to get rid of snoring.*

SHERYL SAYS

I used AI to generate many of the chapter titles and headings in this book and did a little tweaking here and there. But I got some great ideas!

1. "Bright Minds: Empowering Elementary Students through After-School Enrichment"

2. "Exploring Horizons: A Comprehensive After-School Program for Elementary Scholars"

3. "Growing Together: Cultivating Skills and Creativity in Elementary After-School Education"

4. "Pathways to Success: Nurturing Young Minds in our After-School Program"

5. "Beyond the Bell: Enhancing Learning and Well-being in Elementary After-School Activities"

FIGURE 9-1: Titles generated for an elementary school program.

1. "Silent Nights: Investigating Innovative Solutions to Eliminate Snoring"

2. "Sound Sleep Initiative: Advancing Research to Alleviate Snoring Disturbances"

3. "Snore No More: A Scientific Exploration into Effective Anti-Snoring Techniques"

4. "Breath Easy: Pioneering Research to Eradicate Snoring and Improve Sleep Quality"

5. "Snooze Solutions: Advancing Technology and Science to Tackle the Snoring Epidemic"

FIGURE 9-2: Titles generated for research to get rid of snoring.

Crafting an Eye-Catching Visual Identity

As mentioned at the start of this chapter, we do judge books by their covers — and the same goes for grant proposals.

An appealing title-page design can set your proposal apart in a sea of competitors. You can be as creative as you'd like with your proposal cover page so long as it's professional and industry-appropriate. The design should be appealing to the reviewer, while also being functional by building on the proposal's theme.

By leveraging AI for a cover design, you can save time, explore creative options, and ensure your proposal stands out visually to make a strong impression. You don't need to be a graphic designer: The title page can be plain and simple — such as the ideas shown in Figure 9-3 — so long as it is impactful and effective. But if you want to try a little more creativity, Chapter 3 leads you to some visual AI tools.

SHERYL SAYS

Dig deeper into the world of visual design with AI in my book *Business Writing with AI For Dummies* (John Wiley & Sons, Inc., 2024).

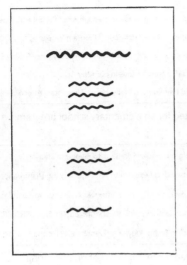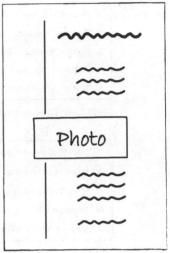

FIGURE 9-3: Two of many ways to present a title page.

Knowing What to Include

REMEMBER

It's important to adhere to any specific formatting requirements or instructions provided by the funding agency. If there aren't any special instructions, here's a good list to follow:

>> **Title of the proposal:** Clearly state the title of your project. It should be concise, descriptive, and original (and yes, as outlined earlier in this chapter, AI can help here).

>> **Name of your organization:** Provide the name of your organization or institution.

>> **Date:** Include the date the proposal is being submitted.

>> **Contact information:** Provide contact details such as project director, the address, phone number, email, and website of your organization.

>> **Funding agency:** Mention the name of the funding agency to whom the proposal is being submitted. (Tip: Make their name and/or logo larger than yours.)

>> **Any other relevant information:** Depending on the specific guidelines provided by the funding agency, you may need to include additional information such as grant identification numbers, project periods, or funding amounts.

SHERYL SAYS

To see some sample title pages, check out https://stock.adobe.com and type in *title pages for a proposal.* You'll get many ideas and can tweak them according to your needs.

Proofreading Very Carefully (or Suffering the Consequences)

WARNING

Never underestimate the power of proofreading when it comes to your title page. One tiny typo might not seem like a big deal, but it could send a negative message to funders — and the loss of your credibility. Double-check everything. Check the accuracy of the information. Check the formatting and layout. Check the clarity and readability. Check against the grant requirements. Check everything! And it's always good to have a fresh pair of (human) eyes take a look — so ask a trusted colleague.

Here's what happens when you don't proofread carefully: During one of my writing workshops, Amanda, a diligent reviewer for grant proposals at Emory University, shared a telling story. She recounted how she was engrossed in reviewing submissions for a significant research project. One particular proposal caught her attention. However, her excitement quickly waned as she scanned the title page and spotted a glaring error — the university's name was misspelled as "Emery" rather than "Emory." Amanda felt that the error indicated a lack of attention to detail, a flaw that could potentially cascade through various phases of the research project. Despite the proposal's potential for harboring groundbreaking ideas, Amanda made the decision to stamp it "Rejected."

AI SPOTLIGHT

Popular proofreading AI tools include Grammarly (https://www.grammarly.com), ProWritingAid (https://prowritingaid.com), and Hemingway Editor https://hemingwayapp.com).

IN THIS CHAPTER

» Understanding the role of the executive summary

» Summing up the value of an executive summary

» Writing your summary after completing your proposal

» Using AI as your summary-writing assistant

» Making your executive summary shine

Chapter 10

Crafting a Captivating Executive Summary

Think of an executive summary like an enticing movie trailer. It provides a tantalizing glimpse of what's to come, highlighting the most compelling aspects in a concise and captivating manner. Just as a movie trailer leaves viewers eager to see the full story unfold on the big screen, a well-crafted executive summary leaves grant reviewers eager to delve deeper into the proposal to uncover all the details and insights it promises. Both aim to grab attention, generate excitement, and leave a lasting impression that compel further engagement.

A killer executive summary gives your proposal a sparkling intro that screams, "Pick me! I'm worth your time!" This can be the difference between your proposal being enthusiastically embraced or lost in the abyss of overlooked proposals. Along with the cover letter (detailed in Chapter 8) and the title page (read more on this in Chapter 9) it serves as the inaugural handshake, setting the stage for the entire proposal.

REMEMBER

In a landscape where time is precious, the executive summary emerges as a time-saving marvel, condensing the essence of the project into a concise narrative. Its strategic significance can't be overstated. It's the platform to showcase the brilliance of your project's vision, objectives, and methodologies.

SHERYL SAYS

In this chapter discover how AI can distill your proposal's essence into a persuasive nutshell. Get ready to master the art of winning over decision makers with a dynamite executive summary right from the get-go!

Recognizing the Allure of the "Appetizer"

Think of this appetizer as setting the stage for the meal to come, making your mouth water in anticipation. You bite into a flawlessly crafted bruschetta — the crunch of the bread, the explosion of fresh tomato, the subtle dance of garlic and basil on your taste buds. With each bite, your anticipation for the main course grows.

REMEMBER

Your executive summary should be the delectable appetizer that leaves the reviewer waiting in anticipation for your main course — the full proposal. In it, be sure to

>> Clearly state the purpose of your proposal.

>> Summarize the main points.

>> Describe any results, conclusions, or recommendations presented in the full proposal.

>> Provide enough information for reviewers to understand the content of the full proposal without having to read it in its entirety.

SHERYL SAYS

During my workshops I'm often asked this question: "Am I allowed to use a chart, table, or graphic in an executive summary?" My answer is Yes. Yes. And Yes. If this will condense critical information and present it at a glance, that's not only allowable, but encouraged. (You'll see an example of this in Figure 10-3, later in this chapter.)

Opening with an inspiring story or a compelling statistic can make your message even more impactful. Just be sure that your statistic is up to date, and double-check the accuracy of anything AI generates. (For more on using stories effectively, check out Chapter 3.)

Understanding the Value of an Executive Summary

With persuasive prowess, the executive summary can convince reviewers of the project's worthiness, leaving an indelible mark in their minds. It's not just a perfunctory component to the overall proposal, but rather the cornerstone of its success, wielding the power to captivate, persuade, and secure the coveted funding.

Imagine busy reviewers, their days a blur of meetings, emails, and urgent tasks, scarcely finding a spare moment to catch their breath, let alone wade through the depths of lengthy proposals. The executive summary is the arsenal of every savvy proposal. It's akin to a superhero's cape, swooping in to rescue time-strapped decision makers by encapsulating all the essential details within just a few succinct pages. Some reviewers will read nothing more than this before passing it to the next level. Make it count!

REMEMBER

If you truly want to captivate busy reviewers, you need more than just a typical summary. You need an action-packed masterpiece. That's where Chapter 4's Kick-Start Brief comes into play. It's your key to unlocking vital insights about your reviewer, empowering you to tailor your summary to perfection. So, take heed and harness the power of this tool. Trust me, it's your golden ticket to seizing the pot of gold.

Writing your Executive Summary Post-Proposal

Just as you wouldn't attempt to write a book report without first delving into its content, crafting an effective executive summary requires a thorough understanding of the proposal. The essence of an executive summary is to distill the core points and overarching message from a more detailed document, so craft it once the rest of your proposal is written. AI can significantly help to streamline the process. A simple prompt for this may read:

> *Create a powerful and engaging 3-page executive summary of the following proposal: [full text]*

AI SPOTLIGHT

AI tools can analyze and synthesize large amounts of information efficiently, identifying the most crucial details and insights within the proposal. This capability ensures that the executive summary accurately captures the essence of the original text while making it concise and accessible for stakeholders. By leveraging AI, you can transform a comprehensive proposal into a focused summary, enhancing communication and decision-making.

Incorporating the Power of AI

AI SPOTLIGHT

Many AI tools offer a summarizing function, but here are a few that are specifically for this purpose:

>> **ClickUp:** https://clickup.com/ai/prompts/executive-summaries

>> **Grammarly:** https://www.grammarly.com

>> **QuillBot:** https://quillbot.com/

>> **SummarizeBot:** https://www.summarizebot.com

Picking Up Tips and Tricks

Crafting an effective executive summary requires skillful synthesis and distilling key insights into a concise format. This section explores invaluable tips and tricks for mastering the essential art of summarization.

Keeping it to the proper length

If you're responding to a Request for Proposal (RFP; see Chapter 11), follow those guidelines. If not, here are some general guidelines to use:

>> If the document is about 50 pages, the summary should be one or two pages.

>> If the document is between 50 and 100 pages, consider an executive summary of two or three pages.

>> If the document is longer than 100 pages, a three- or four-page summary is appropriate.

Failing to adhere strictly to the length described in the funder's guidelines could jeopardize your proposal.

Peppering with keywords

Including keywords in the executive summary is crucial for ensuring that it gets noticed and properly evaluated by the reviewers (which can be a human or an electronic scanner). *Keywords* are specific terms or phrases that highlight the key aspects of your proposed project, such as its goals, target population, methodologies, and expected outcomes. (Learn more in Chapter 6 about how AI can assist with finding keywords.)

Strategically incorporating keywords throughout the proposal helps demonstrate alignment with the funder's priorities and evaluation criteria. This increases the likelihood that your proposal will be accurately matched with the appropriate reviewers and given full consideration.

Using technical terms cautiously

Use technical terms only when you're sure the reviewers reading the report are familiar with them. Not all reviewers have technical backgrounds, so err on the side of being conservative or offer explanations. If you're using initialisms or acronyms, spell them out and follow with the abbreviated form. If you use many such terms, consider including a glossary as part of the back matter. (Back matter is detailed in Chapter 12.)

AI-powered language tools, such as Grammarly or QuillBot, can provide suggestions for simplifying complex language, while AI-based readability checkers can evaluate whether the content is understandable to non-experts.

Showing a positive attitude through your tone

A positive attitude conveys confidence in your ability to execute the project effectively. Your prompt may read:

> *Convey a positive and tone for the following using the active voice and positive words:*

Using positive language such as *will* instead of tentative words such as *would* or *might* demonstrates your commitment and belief in achieving the proposed goals. Here's more that can be accomplished with a positive attitude:

>> **Building excitement and enthusiasm about your project idea.** Incorporating words with positive connotations such as *innovative, exciting,* and *constructive* can influence reviewers to view your proposal more favorably.

>> **Suggesting that you've carefully considered potential challenges and have a solutions-oriented mindset to overcome them.** This reassures reviewers of your preparedness.

>> **Reflecting a can-do spirit and willingness to persevere through the hard work required to successfully implement the proposed activities.** Funders want grantees who will make the most of their investment.

In essence, maintaining an upbeat, confident tone demonstrates to reviewers that you're passionate about your idea, have thoroughly planned for its execution, and have the determination to bring the mission to fruition successful. (There's lots more to discover about tone in Chapter 14.)

SHERYL SAYS

This makes me think of a story in Rosamond Stone Zander and Ben Zander's *The Art of Possibility* (Harvard Business School Press, 2000). It tells of two shoe-factory scouts sent overseas to prospect for business. One scout sends a telegram saying, SITUATION HOPELESS [STOP] NO ONE WEARS SHOES. The other sends a telegram saying, GLORIOUS BUSINESS OPPORTUNITY [STOP] THEY HAVE NO SHOES. If these headlines were presented in an executive summary as "Findings," which would entice the reviewer?

Presenting with impact

In the following figures you see different versions of the same executive summary, before and after some zing has been added. Here is the prompt used for both:

Create an executive summary for the following document. Include an overview, key components, budget, benefits/measuring success, and conclusion. Limit to two pages.

For the "after" version, the following was added to the prompt:

Make this impactful, strong, yet approachable.

Let's consider the differences:

>> **Before: Figures 10-1 and 10-2**

- The opening paragraph is dull. It doesn't offer anything to grab attention.

- Nothing pops out at a glance.

- There's no reason to use numbers as there's no priority.

- The budget section is clunky to follow.

- There's no mention of how success will be measured.

- The conclusion falls flat.

>> **After: Figures 10-3 and 10-4**

- The proposal opens with alarming statistics that grab attention.

- Headlines make key information pop out at a glance.

- Bullets indicate no priority in the listing.

- The budget is displayed as a table, making it easy to follow.

- There are specific guidelines for measuring success.

- The conclusion boasts of how *Together We Can Make a Difference*.

Executive Summary

This proposal is for a 5th- and 6th-grade Nutrition and Exercise Program designed to instill healthy habits in young students through comprehensive education on proper nutrition and exercise. Over the course of four weeks, students will engage in weekly hour-long sessions facilitated by a dedicated healthcare specialist. The program aims to empower students with the knowledge and skills necessary to make informed choices about their diet and physical activity, laying the foundation for a lifetime of wellness.

Key Components:

1. **Curriculum:** The program curriculum covers essential topics such as the importance of balanced nutrition, understanding food groups, portion control, reading food labels, and the benefits of regular exercise. Interactive activities, discussions, and hands-on learning will ensure engagement and comprehension.

2. **Health Care Specialist:** A qualified healthcare specialist will lead each session, providing expert guidance, answering questions, and offering personalized advice to students. Their expertise will ensure that information is accurate, relevant, and tailored to the age group.

3. **Learning Materials:** Each student will receive educational materials such as books, pamphlets, and handouts to supplement the in-class learning experience. These resources will serve as valuable references and reinforcement tools beyond the duration of the program.

4. **Frequency and Duration:** The program will consist of weekly sessions held once a week for four weeks, allowing for consistent exposure to key concepts and sufficient time for understanding and retention.

5. **Budget Allocation:** The budget will primarily cover the expenses associated with hiring a healthcare specialist and purchasing educational materials such as books. By prioritizing these resources, the program ensures quality instruction and impactful learning outcomes.

Budget

1. Healthcare Specialist:
   - Hourly rate for 4 weeks (1 hour per week): $50 per hour
   - Total cost for 4 sessions: $200
2. Educational Materials:
   - Books, pamphlets, and handouts for each student: $1250
3. Administrative Expenses:
   - Miscellaneous expenses (printing, stationery, etc.): $200

So, the total budget for the program would be $1650. Adjustments can be made based on actual rates, number of students, and specific administrative needs.

FIGURE 10-1: Page 1 of an uninteresting executive summary.

Benefits

- **Empowering students to make healthy choices:** By equipping students with knowledge about nutrition and exercise, the program empowers them to make informed decisions that promote their overall well-being.

- **Establishing lifelong habits:** By targeting students at a formative age, the program aims to instill healthy habits that can last a lifetime, reducing the risk of chronic diseases associated with poor nutrition and sedentary lifestyles.

- **Academic and social benefits:** Research shows that healthy eating and regular exercise can improve academic performance, concentration, and social interactions among students. By promoting physical and mental well-being, the program contributes to holistic development.

Conclusion

The 5th- and 6th-grade Nutrition and Exercise Program offers a comprehensive approach to promoting healthy lifestyles among young students. By providing engaging education, expert guidance, and essential resources, the program aims to empower students with the knowledge and skills necessary to prioritize their health and well-being now and in the future.

© *John Wiley & Sons, Inc.*

FIGURE 10-2: Page 2 of an uninteresting executive summary. Yawn!

Executive Summary

It's alarming to realize that childhood obesity and lack of exercise pose significant risks to long-term health and well-being. Obesity rates among children have surged, with approximately 19.3% of children and adolescents in the United States affected. This trend correlates with increased risks of chronic conditions like type 2 diabetes, hypertension, and cardiovascular disease later in life.

Obese children face physical health challenges such as joint problems and asthma, alongside psychological impacts like low self-esteem and depression. Moreover, the economic burden of obesity-related healthcare costs is substantial, totaling billions annually in the United States alone. Addressing these issues early is imperative, as obese children are at risk of reduced life expectancy and academic achievement. Programs promoting proper nutrition and exercise, like the proposed initiative, are vital for mitigating these risks and fostering healthier futures for children. With this pilot program, together we can start to turn this trend around.

Key Components to Creating Healthier Children, Leading to Healthier Adults

Here are the key components that can offer life-changing results:

- **Curriculum:** The program curriculum covers essential topics such as the importance of balanced nutrition, understanding food groups, portion control, reading food labels, and the benefits of regular exercise. Interactive activities, discussions, and hands-on learning will ensure engagement and comprehension.
- **Health Care Specialist:** A qualified healthcare specialist will lead each session, providing expert guidance, answering questions, and offering personalized advice to students. Their expertise will ensure that information is accurate, relevant, and tailored to the age group.
- **Learning Materials:** Each student will receive educational materials such as books, pamphlets, and handouts to supplement the in-class learning experience. These resources will serve as valuable references and reinforcement tools beyond the duration of the program.
- **Frequency and Duration:** The program will consist of weekly sessions held once a week for four weeks, allowing for consistent exposure to key concepts and sufficient time for understanding and retention.

Budget: Pilot Program to Teach 125 Students about Leading Healthier Lives

Budget Item	Cost per Unit	Quantity	Total Cost
Healthcare Specialist	$50/hour	4 hours	$200
Educational Materials	$10/student	125	$1,250
Administrative Expenses	N/A	N/A	$200
Total Budget			**$1,650**

FIGURE 10-3: Page 1 of an engaging executive summary. Much more interesting!

Measuring Success to Determine the Long-Term Impact

By tracking these indicators over a six-month period, educators can assess the impact of the program and determine its success in achieving the goal of promoting healthy eating and exercise habits among 5th- and 6th-grade students. Success could be measured through several key indicators:

- **Behavioral Changes:** Tracking changes in students' behavior related to eating habits and physical activity. This could involve monitoring things like increased consumption of fruits and vegetables, decreased intake of sugary snacks and beverages, and engagement in regular physical activity.

- **Knowledge Retention:** Assessing students' understanding of nutrition and exercise concepts over time to ensure they retain the information learned in the program. This could involve periodic quizzes or tests to gauge their knowledge levels.

- **Physical Health Indicators:** Monitoring physical health indicators such as BMI (Body Mass Index), blood pressure, and cholesterol levels among students to see if there are improvements over time as a result of healthier lifestyle choices.

- **School Performance:** Examining the correlation between healthy habits and academic performance. Research has shown that proper nutrition and regular exercise can positively impact cognitive function and academic achievement.

- **Surveys and Feedback:** Conducting surveys and seeking feedback from students, parents, and teachers to gauge their perceptions of the program and its effectiveness in promoting healthy habits.

Conclusion: Together We Can Make a Difference

Failure to act now could lead to a cascade of detrimental effects. Without intervention, students may face increased risks of obesity, diabetes, and cardiovascular disease, alongside diminished academic performance and lifelong habits of poor health. Mental and emotional well-being may suffer, contributing to societal costs in healthcare and productivity.

Together we can act promptly to instill healthy habits and empower students to lead healthier, happier lives while curbing long-term public health challenges.

FIGURE 10-4: Page 2 of an engaging executive summary. Reviewers will read the whole thing!

WRITING AN ABSTRACT

An abstract is different to an executive summary, yet they can use the same AI tools. To create an abstract, you'll write a prompt that focuses on summarizing the core content of the document in a brief and informative way, often with a focus on research findings, methodologies, or key arguments.

An *abstract* serves as an approximately 100- to 300-word synopsis of the entire proposal. Its purpose is to succinctly convey the key aspects of your project to reviewers and stakeholders, facilitating the evaluation process and promoting the dissemination of your research outcomes. It should address these issues:

- What you intend to do.
- Why the work is important.
- What's already been done.
- How you're going to do the work.

Here are some specific circumstances that call for an abstract:

- **Grant guidelines:** Many grant applications require an abstract as part of their submission requirements. Following these guidelines is crucial for your proposal to be considered.

- **Proposal length limitations:** Grant applications often have strict word or page limits. Including an abstract allows reviewers to quickly grasp the essence of your project without delving into the full proposal immediately.

- **Reviewer's initial assessment:** Reviewers may have to evaluate numerous proposals within a limited time frame. An abstract provides a quick overview, helping them decide whether your project aligns with the grant's objectives and merits further consideration.

- **Clarity and accessibility:** An abstract communicates the essence of your proposal in clear and accessible language. It allows both expert and non-expert readers to understand your project's purpose, methods, and potential impact without having to read the entire proposal.

- **Searchability and indexing:** Abstracts often accompany published research papers or reports funded by grants. Including an abstract ensures that your project is searchable in databases and indexes, increasing its visibility and accessibility to other researchers and stakeholders.

- **Communication with stakeholders:** Granting agencies, potential collaborators, and the public may request project summaries for informational or promotional purposes. An abstract serves as an effective tool for communicating your project's goals and achievements to various stakeholders.

The abstract example shown here aims to unravel complex immunological mechanisms using advanced technologies, with the goal of identifying novel therapeutic targets and revolutionizing immunotherapy for personalized treatment strategies and improved patient outcomes. The limit was 100 words, and the audience was the medical community. This is what AI generated:

Abstract

This proposal aims to clarify intricate immunological pathways crucial for both health and disease. Leveraging existing cutting-edge technologies, we will investigate the dynamic interplay between immune cells, cytokines, and molecular signals to uncover novel targets for therapeutic interventions. By employing advanced imaging techniques and multi-omics analyses, we seek to delineate the complex immune landscape in various pathological conditions, including autoimmune diseases and cancer. Our interdisciplinary approach integrates computational modeling with experimental validation to accelerate the translation of discoveries into clinical applications. Ultimately, this research promises to revolutionize immunotherapy strategies, paving the way for personalized treatments and improved patient outcomes.
(99 words)

The placement of the abstract and the executive summary can vary depending on the specific requirements of the grantor. In some proposals, the abstract may appear before the executive summary, while in others, the executive summary may come first.

Dive into the world of abstract writing with my book *Technical Writing For Dummies*, 2nd Edition (John Wiley & Sons, Inc., 2023). This gem of a book not only unpacks the art of crafting compelling abstracts but also showcases examples to guide you through every nuance of this essential skill.

4

Nailing the Narrative

Sail through the Request for Proposal (RFP) process with AI as your trusty sidekick, making sure you tip the scales in your favor.

Embark on your proposal-writing adventure and discover how AI can supercharge each section, making it leap off the page for the reviewer.

Wow the judges with a presentation that dazzles and seals the deal when you're chosen to represent your organization in the final round of review.

IN THIS CHAPTER

» **Responding to a Request for Proposal**

» **Streamlining the process with AI**

» **Making contact with the funder**

» **Maximizing your chances of success**

» **Making sure you cover all bases**

Chapter **11**

Navigating a Request for Proposal

A *Request for Proposal* (RFP) is like a casting call for a block-buster movie. The film studio (organization) puts out a detailed script (RFP) that includes the plot, the roles, and what they're looking for in actors and crew. This script is sent to a bunch of talent agencies (potential vendors or contractors) who then prepare and submit their auditions (proposals). Each show-cases their unique take on how they would bring the project to life, and the studio (reviewer) evaluates all the submissions to choose the best.

This chapter helps you navigate the RFP process with precision and purpose, leveraging the tools to illuminate the path ahead.

Finding Funders

Chapter 16 goes into greater detail about finding funders in the United States and abroad, but here's a little taster for find-ing funding:

>> **Applying cold.** This means reaching out to potential funders without a prior relationship or introduction, often through

unsolicited proposals or requests. This involves researching potential funders, understanding their priorities and guidelines, and submitting unsolicited proposals or grant applications. The advantage is a broad range of funding sources, but you must initiate the search.

>> **Responding to RFPs.** When individuals or organizations respond to RFPs, they're addressing specific funding opportunities that have been formally announced by the funding source. RFPs typically outline the objectives, eligibility criteria, and submission requirements. The advantage is the funder has provided a specific framework to follow; however, the competition may be intense.

AI can be incredibly valuable in locating RFPs by automating the search process and providing tailored recommendations. Here's how:

>> Parsing through vast amounts of text data, such as websites, forums, and databases to identify RFP-related content.

>> Recognizing keywords and phrases commonly associated with RFPs across various industries and sectors.

>> Having been trained on historical RFP data to learn patterns and trends in RFP announcements. This allows AI models to predict the likelihood of new RFPs appearing based on factors such as industry, location, and previous procurement history.

>> Setting up systems to send personalized alerts and notifications whenever new RFPs matching specific criteria are detected.

>> Integrating with existing databases and procurement systems to streamline the RFP discovery process.

Thinking of AI as Your Personal Agent

AI can act as your personal agent in the RFP process by quickly analyzing proposals, matching them with your criteria, and highlighting the best options. It streamlines the entire workflow, saving you time and ensuring you find the most suitable vendors or solutions efficiently. Check out Loopio (https://learn.loopio.com/rfp-response-software), QorusDocs (https://www.qorusdocs.com), and Responsive (https://www.responsive.io).

Contacting Funders Beforehand

While it's not feasible on every occasion, contacting the funder before submitting your proposal demonstrates your commitment, professionalism, and willingness to engage collaboratively and build rapport. Finding the right person can provide valuable information and insights that significantly improve your chances of success in securing the funding. Make sure to prepare your questions beforehand. For example:

>> What are the primary objectives of the funding opportunity? Can you provide more detail or examples of the outcomes the funder hopes to achieve through this funding?

>> Are there any specific requirements regarding the type of organization, geographic location, or project focus?

>> Are there specific funding amounts allocated for different types of projects or activities?

>> When can applicants expect to receive notification of funding decisions?

>> What criteria will be used to evaluate proposals? How important are factors such as innovation, scalability, community impact, or previous experience?

>> Are there any restrictions or limitations on how the funds can be used? Are there any activities or expenses that are not eligible for funding?

>> What are the reporting requirements for funded projects? How often are progress reports or financial reports required, and what information should be included in these reports?

>> Are there resources or guidance materials that can help applicants prepare strong proposals?

>> Are partnerships or collaborations encouraged or required for this funding opportunity?

>> Are there any specific expectations regarding the involvement of other organizations or stakeholders?

>> Can they provide examples of past projects that have been funded through similar opportunities?

>> Are there any success stories or lessons learned that can provide insights for prospective applicants?

Finding the right person to contact within the organization is helpful for getting the information you need. You can identify the right person in the following ways:

>> Reviewing the RFP document

>> Visiting the funder's website

>> Networking

>> Using social media and professional platforms such as LinkedIn

>> Checking previous communications

>> Calling the funder's main telephone number

REMEMBER

Regardless of the initial method of contact, remember the importance of following up. For example, if you reach out by phone, sending a follow-up email to summarize the conversation can create a written record and make you more memorable. AI can be of great value when drafting your follow-up.

AI SPOTLIGHT

AI can also help by digging into each funder's past projects and interests, to help you come up with thoughtful, on-point questions that show you've done your homework and are genuinely interested in their priorities.

Anchoring the Academy Award

AI SPOTLIGHT

Integrating AI into the RFP process can streamline tasks and boost accuracy, ultimately enhancing the quality of your proposal. This efficiency not only improves your chances in competitive bidding but can also elevate your submission to a level worthy of acclaim. Imagine it as having a secret weapon to help you secure that Academy Award of contract awards. Here's how:

>> **Analyzing and extracting key information from the RFP document.** It can then highlight critical requirements, evaluation criteria, and submission guidelines, making it easier to focus on essential details.

>> **Generating a list of questions or clarifications based on the text of the RFP.** It can also assist in drafting clear, concise inquiries to seek clarifications from the issuing agency.

>> **Tailoring your proposal by comparing RFP objectives with your proposed solution.** AI algorithms can help align your response to meet the specific needs and goals outlined in the RFP.

>> **Automating the application of the correct format and structure.** It can ensure that your proposal adheres to all specified sections, headings, page limits, and attachment requirements.

>> **Analyzing competitor proposals or market data to identify your unique strengths and value propositions.** It can suggest how best to articulate what sets your proposal apart.

>> **Drafting content that's detailed yet concise.** It can also assist in creating visuals and diagrams to illustrate key points effectively.

>> **Collating and presenting your relevant experience, qualifications, and past successes.** It can further generate summaries of client references and case studies that align with the project requirements.

>> **Providing AI-driven project management tools to track deadlines and send reminders to ensure timely submission.** It can also help organize and prepare files for submission according to RFP specifications.

>> **Performing thorough reviews of your proposal, identifying errors, inconsistencies, and areas for improvement.** It can suggest revisions to enhance clarity and effectiveness.

AI can also assist in preparing for presentations by analyzing your proposal and suggesting key points to emphasize. It can create compelling visual aids and practice simulations to improve your delivery. (Learn more about preparing for the presentation in Chapter 13.)

Using a Match-Up Approach with the Help of AI

SHERYL
SAYS

One of my clients kept missing out on funding worth millions and were adrift as to what kept going wrong. Their proposals were being turned down because funders claimed they hadn't answered all the questions requested in the RFP. But here's the kicker: They actually had answered all the questions. The problem was, the answers were buried deep within the proposal. They asked for my help. To solve this problem and to make sure this didn't happen with the proposal I wrote for them, I crafted an annotated table of contents (TOC) with the help of AI, as demonstrated in Figure 11-1. I matched each requested item with its page number, using the exact language in the RFP. The proposal suddenly became a beacon of clarity in a sea of confusion. With this simple inclusion, funders could easily find the answers they sought. And the tide for this company turned. The proposal immediately garnered attention, swiftly leading to the company's securing not only that funding, but funding for several other projects by using the match-up approach.

RFP Item Requested	Page Number
Project Understanding	23
Methodology Overview	24
Task Breakdown	25
Resource Allocation	27
Risk Management	29
Quality Assurance	31
Communication & Reporting	33
Evaluation & Feedback	34

FIGURE 11-1: An annotated TOC matching each item in the RFP with its page number in the proposal.

AI SPOTLIGHT

Here are three of the many TOC generators to choose from: Notion (https://www.notion.so), Chrome Web Store (https://chromewebstore.google.com), and Canva (https://www.canva.com/create/table-of-contents).

IN THIS CHAPTER

» Using AI as your proposal-writing ally

» Recognizing funders as partners

» Looking at the different sections of a grant proposal

» Giving your proposal a final read through

» Following up with a funder

Chapter **12**

Unlocking Funding Doors: Writing Stellar Proposals

A s the clock strikes "Time to fund your dream project" you find yourself faced with the task of writing a grant proposal. This chapter takes you through the frenzy of writing a grant proposal, where the pen is mightier than the sword, and the grant proposal is your trusty machete. So sharpen your pencil and ready your mind, for you're about to embark on a quest to unlock what it takes to prepare a funding-worthy masterpiece. From crafting a powerful executive summary that leaves the grant reviewer wanting more (like a cliffhanger in a thrilling novel) to meticulously outlining your project's objectives and budget, you'll be equipped with the knowledge and AI tools necessary to present your vision in a way that resonates with potential funders.

REMEMBER

The extent of information you include in each section is relative to how large the project is and how much money you request. This chapter includes a list of the typical parts of a large grant. Yours may not require all the inclusions. And before your forge ahead with writing a proposal, make sure to fill out the Kick-Start Brief found in Chapter 4. By following it, you'll build a connection with the reviewers, make it clear why your project is important. It can help to turn your ideas into a strong case for getting funded.

This chapter takes you through every essential step of writing a successful grant proposal., Buckle up and get ready to elevate your game to pro status to bring home that pot of gold!

Weaving AI into the Process

As you read through this chapter, you'll discover many ways that AI can be an indispensable ally. Sometimes I nudge you toward revisiting pertinent chapters in this book, and at other times I'll introduce you to AI tools tailored for a specific use. And yet other times, there'll be no AI reference because the task is a DYI-er (do-it-yourself-er) that needs to be addressed by writer intelligence (WI) — that's you and the proposal-writing team.

If you're using any of the tools mentioned elsewhere in this book, be sure to adjust the tone and content to ensure that it aligns with your organization's voice.

Building Partners, Not Grantors

Envision the intended grantor as your spirited partner in a grand quest — not as a mere benefactor. This will open up the realm of possibilities. Chapter 3 describes storytelling, but for now picture this: You (the valiant grant seeker) and the grantor (a fellow adventurer) are standing shoulder to shoulder, fueled by shared purpose and determination. Together, you forge a path toward your noble goal, weaving dreams into reality, and leaving bureaucratic hurdles in your wake. Paint a vivid picture of how your organization and the grantor will waltz through challenges, hand in hand. The grant proposal becomes more than words; it can become a saga of shared valor, an epic of mutual triumph!

Recognizing the funder not merely as a financial supporter, but as a valued partner in the venture is crucial for fostering mutual collaboration, shared ownership, and sustained impact. Here are some examples of partnership phrases generated by AI that will help the funder feel involved in the project from the get-go:

Prompt: *Give me 3 examples of phrases to let the funder know that we want a partnership, not just funds.*

AI's responses:

Your support as our partner in this project is invaluable, and we look forward to working hand in hand to address [specific issue] to make a meaningful impact.

Together, we have the opportunity to make a real difference. Your partnership is not only about funding; it's about joining forces to tackle [specific challenge] and create lasting social impact.

As your partner, we are committed to transparency, open communication, and shared decision-making. Together we can achieve far more than we ever could alone.

Breaking Down the Sections of a Grant Proposal

A grant proposal should be presented in several sections to ensure that it's clear, comprehensive, and easy to navigate — ultimately enhancing its effectiveness and impact. This improved readability helps reviewers focus on content.

Throughout this section you'll find examples that plug into certain aspects of a grant proposal. They were generated by AI based on my prompts and demonstrate a grant proposal requesting $150,000 to build an inner-city playground on a currently empty lot. The proposal highlights how the funds will benefit the children, the parents, and the community.

Section 1: The beginning

Provide the hook. This is the section where you have the opportunity to grab the grant reviewer's attention. Let them know they're about to read a very interesting and worthwhile proposal. Don't promise the moon, but be honest and realistic.

Include the title page, table of contents, and executive summary. Although the cover letter (discussed in Chapter 8) is the first thing the reviewer sees, it's not considered part of "the beginning." You could say it begins the beginning.

Cover letter (a.k.a. transmittal letter)

You'll submit a proposal in one of three ways: online, email, or snail mail. Every one of these requires a cover letter. If you're sending an actual letter, prepare it on your letterhead. Otherwise, you'll send it electronically, like the one in Figure 12-1. It's the first thing a grant reviewer sees and will be the basis of their first impression. It should convey the following in no more than three paragraphs:

>> A brief story that will appeal to hearts and minds. (Check out Chapter 3).

>> The undertaking and two of its major selling points.

>> The reasons you're applying for a grant.

>> An explanation that you're looking to partner with them, not just take their funding.

Dear Mr. Jameson:

In the heart of Yonkers, NY, an inner-city playground has sparked a remarkable transformation. The once barren and lifeless lot has been reborn as a lively gathering place for all to enjoy. Children now explore the colorful structures, sparking their imaginations, while families come together in shared joy and unity. This playground has cultivated friendships, improved children's health, and reignited hope, embodying the power of collective action and the endless possibilities of community investment.

The primary objective of requesting $150,000 is to replicate that effort on another empty lot — to establish a secure, inclusive, and engaging environment where children and families can partake in active play, foster social bonds, and promote physical and mental wellness. Located strategically in a central locale of the city, the playground will be easily accessible to families residing in nearby neighborhoods.

We invite you to join us in championing this important cause. Together we can create a vibrant hub for recreation and social interaction, enriching the lives of individuals across our community. The playground will not only serve as a haven for fun and laughter but also as a catalyst for promoting health, inclusivity, and community cohesion. Your support will not only contribute to the physical infrastructure but also to the social fabric of our community, nurturing a brighter, more interconnected future for all.

Thank you for your consideration.

Most sincerely,

FIGURE 12-1: Sample cover letter generated by AI and sent via email.

Writing the cover letter after completing the proposal is more effective because you can tailor it to the specifics emphasizing key points, and address any specific requirements or preferences outlined by the grant provider. Plus, once you've finished the proposal, AI can assist in crafting the cover letter, streamlining the process and making a dynamic first impression. Learn more about the cover letter and relevant AI tools in Chapter 8.

Title page

Specific requirements for a grant proposal title page may vary depending on the granting agency. If the funder gives specifications, carefully review them to ensure that the title page is formatted correctly and includes all the required information. If it's left to your discretion, include these in the following in this order:

» Title of project (in a font larger than the rest)

» Funder's name, address, and telephone number

» Your organization's name and contact information

» Submission date

AI SPOTLIGHT

Never underestimate the value of a dynamic title and title page. AI can be a valuable assistant in creating each. Learn more in Chapter 9 about the tools that can be of value.

Table of contents

Creating a table of contents (TOC) for a proposal of more than 10 pages is essential to provide an organized overview of the proposal's structure and contents. This allows grant reviewers to quickly locate specific sections or information, providing a clear road map for navigating the entire document. Additionally, it demonstrates the proposal writer's thoroughness and attention to detail, which can positively influence reviewers' perceptions of the proposal's quality and professionalism.

REMEMBER

When responding to a lengthy Request for Proposal (RFP) (more about RFPs in Chapter 11), consider including a detailed TOC of where the grant reviewers can find everything they've requested. If you use Microsoft as your word processor, check out https:// www.ablebits.com/office-addins-blog/create-table-of-contents-word to discover how it can generate a TOC. If you use another word processor, check its capabilities via an online search.

AI SPOTLIGHT

TOC-generation AI tools include AIWriter (https://ai-writer.com) and Coggle (https://coggle.it).

Executive summary

Nearly 90 percent of all funding decisions are made before the potential reviewer finishes reading the executive summary!

In the first paragraph, set the stage for the story. The "who, where, what, when, why, and how" that gives a hint of direction. During this time the grant reviewer is trying get some context, to understand where you're headed, and how they fit into the journey. Make this section concise, persuasive, engaging, and include charts or tables where appropriate. Limit this to no more than three or four pages. See an example in Figure 12-2.

Executive Summary

This proposal seeks funding totaling $150,000 to facilitate the construction of an inner-city playground in Yonkers, NY. The primary aim of this project is to establish a secure, inclusive, and engaging environment where children and families within our community can partake in active play, cultivate social bonds, and enhance both physical and mental wellness.

Situated strategically in a central part of the city, the proposed playground will be conveniently accessible to families residing in nearby neighborhoods. Its design will encompass a diverse array of play structures, meticulously curated to cater to children of all ages and abilities. Envisioned features include swings, slides, climbing apparatus, and interactive elements, ensuring a stimulating and enjoyable experience for every visitor.

By investing in this project, we aspire to foster a vibrant hub for recreation and social interaction, enriching the lives of individuals across our community. This playground will not only serve as a haven for fun and laughter but also as a catalyst for promoting health, inclusivity, and community cohesion.

We invite you to join us in championing this initiative, empowering our city's youth, and nurturing a brighter, more interconnected future for all.

FIGURE 12-2: Executive summary generated by AI.

Don't write the executive summary until you've written the proposal. Here's what to include:

>> Introduction of purpose

>> Project description

>> Methods and approach

>> Expected outcomes and impact

>> Budget

>> Relevant experience

>> Sustainability

>> Conclusion

Be sure to check out Chapter 10 to discover tips, tricks, and AI tools to assist with your executive summary.

Section 2: The middle

This is the juicy, savory essence, the prime cut of content where you educate and powerfully convince. It should be informative, persuasive, and assuring. Lavish this section with stories and testimonials to let them know how their much-needed funds will be wisely spent, based on your past (or anticipated) success. These stories may show how your team was so efficient they completed the project ahead of schedule and under budget, or whatever your success story is.

REMEMBER

Incorporate your capacity to navigate the project's journey until completion, showcasing your organization's fervor for both your dedication to the project and its beneficiaries.

Include in this section the following: purpose (or introduction), problem statement, goals and objectives, budgetary needs, timetable, sustainability, promotion, target population, best practices, and qualifications.

Purpose (or introduction)

In one page or less, introduce the following:

>> **Concept:** How this project fits into the philosophy and mission of the funder and your organization.

>> **Key elements of the program:** This includes the nature of project, timetable, anticipated outcomes, and staffing needs.

>> **Overview of the financials:** At this stage you may not be able to pinpoint all expenses, but you can present broad outlines.

In Figure 12-3, notice how graphics can play a critical part. Who with a heart could say "No" to joining your cause and funding the project to create those happy little faces?

Problem statement

The problem statement in a proposal should strongly and succinctly describe the issues or challenges the proposed project aims to address.

Purpose: Benefitting Children, Parents, and Community

We are requesting funding in the amount of $150,000 to support the construction of an inner-city playground in Yonkers, NY. This playground will provide a safe, accessible, and inclusive space for children and families in our community to engage in active play, foster social connections, and promote physical and mental well-being. The proposed playground will be located in a central area of the city, easily accessible to families living in nearby neighborhoods. It will feature a variety of play structures suitable for children of all ages and abilities, including swings, slides, climbing structures, and interactive play elements.

This playground would offer numerous benefits. For children, it would provide opportunities for physical development through active play, fostering motor skills and overall health. Additionally, playgrounds support cognitive development by encouraging imaginative and exploratory play, enhancing problem-solving skills and creativity. Interacting with peers on the playground also helps children develop crucial social skills such as cooperation and communication.

For parents, this facility would offer peace of mind with safe environments for their children to play freely, promoting relaxation. This playground would also serve as a hub for community engagement, allowing parents to connect with others and build support networks. Furthermore, spending time together at the playground strengthens parent-child bonds, enriching family relationships and promoting overall well-being.

Together, we can turn this vision into reality and create a space where children can laugh, play, and thrive.

Jackie Davies/Adobe Stock Photos, hedgehog94/Adobe Stock Photos

FIGURE 12-3: Vision for the project with before and after visuals.

AI SPOTLIGHT

The following was generated by AI using a negative approach to appeal for the funding by highlighting what will happen if we don't act:

Prompt: *Write two brief paragraphs on how the absence of playground equipment in a vacant inner-city lot negatively impacts the community. Feel free to elaborate. Make it compelling.*

AI's response: *The absence of a suitable playground in our inner-city neighborhood has created a significant gap in recreational opportunities for our community's children, resulting in limited physical activity and social interaction. The vacant lot currently serves as a stark reminder of this deficiency, offering no safe and constructive space for children to play and thrive.*

This lack of recreational infrastructure not only hinders the physical and social development of our children but also contributes to a sense of neglect within the community, exacerbating concerns about safety and well-being among parents and residents alike.

Goals and objectives

Make sure your goals are SMART (specific, measurable, achievable, relevant, and time-bound). Express them in a powerful sentence to spark the imagination of the reviewers. Support your goal with the long- and short-term objectives, which are the steps along the way. Include the following:

>> Measurable milestones you will reach in meeting those goals and objectives.

>> How you will know that you're making progress towards your goals and objectives.

Budgetary needs

You probably won't be able to pin down all the expenses until the details and timing are finalized. For the purpose of writing the grant, sketch out the broad outlines of the budget. Be sure the costs are in proportion to the outcomes you anticipate. Also, mention funding from other sources, such as volunteer services or other funders.

If it appears that the costs will be prohibitive, scale back your plans or adjust them to remove expenses that aren't cost effective.

AI not only prepared the table you see in Figure 12-4, but it provided the allocation for funding, too. Most of the AI tools mentioned in Chapter 1 can prepare tables. In addition to preparing the table — without prompting — the AI tool showed potential funders for this project as shown in Figure 12-5. Voila!

Timetable

State how long should this project should take and the steps along the way. If your grant proposal is short and the project is a simple one, you may say, *The project will start within 30 days of receiving the funding and will be completed six months from the start date.*

Item	Cost
Playground equipment	$100,000
Site preparation and installation	$30,000
Landscaping and amenities	$15,000
Contingency fund	$5,000
Total	$150,000

FIGURE 12-4: Budget presented as a table by AI.

The search results indicate that there are various grants and funding sources available to help cover the costs of playground equipment and related projects. Some key points:

- The York County, VA Capital Improvements Program allocates funding for the repair and maintenance of recreational facilities, including playgrounds. [1]

- The Playground Equipment Grants and Stimulus Guide provides an overview of national and state-level grants that can be used for playground projects. [2] [3] [6]

- Potential funding sources include the National Parks Service Land and Water Conservation Fund, the Finish Line Youth Foundation, the Bureau of Land Management, and the PNC Foundation, among others. [4]

The total cost of $150,000 for the playground equipment, site preparation, landscaping, and contingency fund appears to be within the range of funding available through these various grant programs. [1] [2] [3] [4]

FIGURE 12-5: Additional funding information provided by the AI tool.

AI SPOTLIGHT

AI can help with scheduling by anticipating potential delays, recommending workarounds, helping to schedule meetings, in addition to aiding with other time-management functions. Figure 12-6 showing the timetable for completing the playground was prepared by AI.

If you want to display this information graphically, these tools can help:

>> **Atlassian:** https://www.atlassian.com

>> **Gantt.com:** https://www.gantt.com

>> **Miro:** https://miro.com

>> **Monday.com:** https://monday.com

6–8 Months before opening

- Determine who will use the playground and their needs
- Assess the playground site and analyze space considerations
- Decide on a budget and explore funding options
- Choose playground equipment that fits the space and budget

4–6 Months before opening

- Obtain necessary permits from the city
- Prepare the site by improving drainage, slope, etc.
- Order playground equipment and surfacing materials

2–3 Months before opening

- Receive and store playground equipment and materials
- Prepare the site for installation, including groundwork

1 Month before opening

- Install playground equipment and surfacing
- Complete any additional site work like lighting, sidewalks

2 Weeks before opening

- Conduct final inspection and make any necessary repairs
- Prepare for grand opening celebration

Opening Day

- Celebrate the new playground with the community!

The key is to allow 6–8 months for the entire process, from planning to installation. Obtaining permits, preparing the site, and manufacturing custom equipment can each take 4–6 weeks. Ordering equipment early is critical, as lead times are typically 3–6 months. With proper planning and a realistic timeline, a basic inner-city playground can be built and ready for the community to enjoy

© *John Wiley & Sons, Inc.*

FIGURE 12-6: Timetable for completion of playground.

Sustainability

Assuming the program proves successful and the initial funding ends, the focus should be on ensuring its sustainability. This involves developing a plan for the program to eventually run independently and seeking alternative funding sources if necessary. Additionally, it may be beneficial to explore the possibility of obtaining further support from the current grantor to continue the program's impact and success.

AI can aid with sustainability by optimizing resource use, predicting and mitigating environmental impacts, and improving efficiency in energy and waste management. It can also enhance decision-making through data analysis, support the development of sustainable technologies, and monitor and analyze environmental changes for better planning and adaptation.

Promotion

Outline your plans for promoting the program. Through a public relations campaign? Through community affairs organizations? In professional journals? If you have existing marketing literature, send it along.

AI can be a valuable partner in developing promotional strategies. This can include community events and fundraisers, media coverage, visual collateral, and social media coverage. You could ask your AI tool to flesh each one out and come up with a comprehensive promo plan.

Target population

If your target population is a factor, detail who they are. For example, an organization doing research on a specific disease may do a study whose target population is a certain ethnic group of certain ages. Do this by

>> Gathering relevant data and statistics that support the need for the proposed project or program. This will help you demonstrate the significance and impact of your work.

>> Highlighting any existing collaborations or partnerships with organizations or stakeholders that have experience working with the target population and your commitment to working collaboratively and leveraging existing resources and expertise . . . in addition to sharing your findings.

AI can help identify the target population by analyzing large sets of data to find patterns and trends. It can segment populations based on various factors like demographics or behaviors, and predict which groups are most likely to benefit from a program or product. This makes targeting more precise and effective.

Best practices

How will you share the success of your project with other organizations or communities? Will you share the "lessons learned" so others can learn from what worked and what didn't work? Also, what best practices from others will you apply to this process?

AI
SPOTLIGHT

AI can identify best practices by: analyzing successful examples and patterns; evaluating clarity, organization, and relevance; and comparing the proposal's content against industry standards and benchmarks.

Qualifications

REMEMBER

Many groups are vying for the same dollars. Detail why you're more qualified or better able to reach your goal:

>> If you've had a breakthrough or success on something similar in the past, be specific about how you met your goals.

>> Use percentages and dollar amounts. They can be powerful.

>> If you have notable people who'll lead the charge, include a brief paragraph about them, and prepare resumes to appear in the appendixes (see the next section).

AI
SPOTLIGHT

Use the assistance of AI to generate any of these accomplishments by prompting:

Amplify the following to make them sound outstanding: [Text].

You can use any of the AI tools mentioned in Chapter 1 for this.

Section 3: The conclusion and back matter

REMEMBER

The conclusion offers you one last chance to convince the grantor to fund your initiative. Here are some tips to help you craft a memorable conclusion:

>> Restate the problem

>> Recap the objectives

- >> Showcase the feasibility
- >> Highlight innovation
- >> Express confidence
- >> Throw in a testimonial from a person or group who benefitted in the past.
- >> Call to action with the grantor as a partner, not a funder

Included in this section are the appendixes and glossary. However, back matter can also include references, bibliographies, supplementary documents, case studies or examples, additional budget details, legal or compliance information, special certifications, contact information, or anything else that didn't appear in other parts of the proposal. This gives reviewers access to all relevant information they need to make an informed decision.

Appendixes

This is one more opportunity for sharing stories. Consider including a section titled "More About Our Successes" or "More About Our Team." These success stories can be lengthier (a page or more) and can include case studies. Even though this isn't a standard part of a grant proposal, it adds credibility and sets you apart from the competition.

REMEMBER

This section is *not* an afterthought or a place to stick random information. It should be a carefully curated section that adds depth and validation to your proposal. Be mindful of keeping to what's absolutely necessary to round out your proposal. You don't want to overwhelm.

Glossary

Throughout the grant proposal, keep industry-specific terms, acronyms, or initialisms to a minimum. Although there's no magic number, include a glossary when you have many terms you think the reviewers may not be familiar with. This is truly a judgment call.

AI SPOTLIGHT

AI can help to tailor the definitions according to your reviewer's needs, ranging from simple to technical language. But always remember, it's WI that must give the proposal a final blessing.

REMEMBERING THE DO'S AND DON'TS

As you finalize your proposal, keep these key guidelines in mind to enhance your submission and avoid common mistakes:

- Do consider ethical considerations such as honesty and accuracy, conflicts of interest, responsible conduct of research, inclusivity and diversity, protection of names, animal welfare, environmental impact, community engagement and stakeholder consultation, data management and sharing, and intellectual property rights.

- Do describe your program with facts, statistics, and passion using action-packed words such as *achieving, cooperating, enhancing, establishing, existing, expanding, overall, strategies,* and the like.

- Do present your goals with visionary language and your objectives with measurable terms using high-performance words such as *decreasing, delivering, developing, establishing, improving, increasing,* and *producing.*

- Don't beat around the bush about future funding. Use words such as *creating future fundraising partners, inviting more external funding sources, local fundraising, seeking to identify more stakeholders,* to name a few.

- Don't use statements that say the obvious such as *illiteracy is a barrier to employment, clean water is essential, many of the world's population live in chronic hunger, homelessness is a serious issue,* and similar.

Making a List and Checking It Twice

Before submitting your proposal give it one — or two! — final checks over. In addition to proofreading and editing your proposal for obvious errors, here's a checklist of things to look for that only WI can detect:

☐ **Overall Structure and Flow**
- Is the proposal organized logically with clear sections (such as the introduction, objectives, methods, and budget)?

- Does each section flow smoothly into the next, providing a coherent narrative?
- ☐ **Storytelling**
  - Did you include stories that tug at heartstrings and open wallets?
  - Did you pepper the proposal with story testimonials?
- ☐ **Clarity and Conciseness**
  - Are technical terms defined or explained appropriately?
  - Have you avoided unnecessary jargon that could confuse reviewers?
- ☐ **Grammar and Punctuation**
  - Are sentences grammatically correct?
  - Are punctuation marks (such as commas and semicolons) used correctly?
- ☐ **Consistency**
  - Are formatting styles (for example, headings, font sizes, and spacing) consistent throughout the document?
  - Are abbreviations and acronyms consistently used and defined?
- ☐ **Accuracy and Completeness**
  - Have you verified all facts, figures, and statistical data cited in the proposal?
  - Are all references properly cited, and do they support your arguments?
- ☐ **Readability and Presentation**
  - Is the text easy to read, with clear and concise language?
  - Have you used bullet points, tables, and effectively to present complex information?
- ☐ **Persuasiveness and Impact**
  - Does the proposal effectively convey the significance and potential impact of the project?
  - Have you clearly outlined how the project aligns with the grant's objectives and priorities?
- ☐ **Review for Specific Requirements**

- Have you followed the grant application guidelines and included all required elements (for example, project summary, budget, and supporting documents)?
- Have you addressed any specific criteria or questions outlined in the grant application?

❏ **Peer Review and Feedback**
- Have you sought feedback from colleagues or mentors on the content and structure of the proposal?
- Have you incorporated constructive feedback to strengthen the proposal?

❏ **Final Proofreading**
- Have you carefully proofread the entire proposal for typos, spelling errors, and formatting inconsistencies?
- Consider using spellcheck tools and reading the proposal aloud to catch any remaining issues.

By following this checklist, you can ensure that your grant proposal is well-polished, coherent, and compelling for reviewers.

Following Up After Submitting Your Proposal

Following up with a funder after submitting a grant proposal is crucial for several reasons: It demonstrates your interest and commitment, builds a relationship, increases your visibility, and shows professionalism.

REMEMBER

Prepare a concise message expressing gratitude for the opportunity to apply and politely request an update on the status of your application. Being patient and understanding throughout the process can help maintain a positive impression while ensuring your inquiry is productive. For example:

> **Prompt:** *Please write a friendly 2-paragraph message inquiring about the status of my proposal. Ask for an update and when I may expect to hear.*

AI's response:

I am reaching out to inquire about the status of our grant application submitted on [date]. We're excited about the opportunity to partner with you and are eager to hear any updates you might have. Do you have any idea when that may be?

Thank you so much for your time and consideration. If there's any additional information you need, please let me know.

Most sincerely,

Knowing how to follow up

Here are some ways to follow up:

>> **Emailing:** Send a polite and concise email to the contact person or the appropriate department. Express gratitude for the opportunity to submit the proposal, reiterate your enthusiasm for the project, and politely inquire about the status of your application. AI can draft this follow-up.

>> **Making a phone call:** Follow up with a phone call if a number was provided. A phone call allows for more immediate feedback and clarification. Make sure to prepare a script or talking points beforehand and be respectful of the recipient's time. Again, AI can help formulate questions.

>> **Requesting a meeting:** If feasible, request a meeting to discuss your proposal in more detail. This can provide an opportunity for deeper engagement and to address any concerns the funder may have.

>> **Using social media:** Engage with the funder on social media platforms such as LinkedIn or X. This can help keep your project on their radar and demonstrate your proactive approach.

>> **Attending events:** If the funder hosts or attends events, consider attending to network and make a personal connection. This can help strengthen your relationship with the funder and increase the chances of your proposal being considered.

>> **Sending additional information:** If the funder requests additional information or documentation (or if you just want to send something to remind them of your proposal), be sure to provide them promptly. This demonstrates your responsiveness and willingness to collaborate.

Knowing when to follow up

It's important to check the specified time frame for hearing back on applications and adhere to any guidelines regarding follow-ups provided by the grantor. Typically, it's advisable to wait two to four weeks after the application deadline before politely reaching. Some funders post updates on their websites.

REMEMBER

Waiting can be tough but it's all part of the process. Stay optimistic — sometimes the best things take a little longer to come together. Your patience and persistence will pay off. If not this time, you can always try again.

Chapter **13**

Appearing as a Finalist to Shoot for the Gold

After undergoing rigorous rounds of reviews, your proposal emerges as a finalist! Now, as you prepare to take center stage either in person or via a video link, all eyes are on you! This presentation is your moment to captivate the reviewers with your charisma, intellect, passion, and conviction. Your proposal must win over the grant reviewing panel and secure vital funding through its innovative storytelling and emotional depth.

SHERYL SAYS

When your proposal enters the final showdown, prepare a presentation to dazzle the judges and seal the deal! With AI as your sidekick, this chapter covers everything from crafting captivating stories to polishing your slides to perfection. Get ready to shine like a star and leave a lasting impression that's impossible to resist!

Peeking Behind the Curtain of the Review Process

Review processes can vary greatly, akin to the assorted flavors in a box of chocolates. Factors such as the funding body, the nature of the grant, and the expertise of the reviewers contribute to this range. As the review process unfolds, proposals are progressively scrutinized, leading to heightened competition as weaker submissions are weeded out. The following steps are the fullest extent of a review process:

1. **Initial screening**
2. **Peer review**
3. **Panel review or committee evaluation**
4. **Finalists presentations (optional by funder)**
5. **Grant awarded**

Remembering That AI Can Help

AI SPOTLIGHT

AI can be a valuable tool in preparing for and delivering a presentation as a finalist for a grant. One of the key ways is generating content with tools such as HyperWrite (https://www.hyperwriteai.com/aitools/ai-speech-writer) and Verble (https://www.verble.app). Also, tools such as Presentr (https://www.thepresentr.me) and Ovation (https://www.ovationvr.com) can provide simulated practice sessions where you can rehearse your presentation. They can offer feedback on aspects such as pacing, tone, and clarity, helping you refine your delivery.

Other opportunities to lean on AI are highlighted elsewhere in this chapter.

Assessing the Review Panel

Typically, you might not know the people on the review panel, but you can often infer general characteristics based on the panel's purpose or the field of study. For example, if it's a grant proposal for scientific research, you can assume panel members have expertise in that scientific area. Understanding the general background and interests of your audience helps you tailor your presentation effectively. You can prepare by understanding the criteria, highlighting key points, anticipating questions, and practicing your pitch.

AI SPOTLIGHT

Tools such as QuillBot, (https://quillbot.com) and Altair RapidMiner (https://altair.com/altair-rapidminer) can assist in several ways:

>> Simulating questions and providing feedback

>> Refining your content to ensure that it is well-organized and compelling

>> Data mining

>> Acting as a virtual assistant to provide practice sessions and feedback

Crafting Your Presentation's Message

Crafting your message for the panel requires careful consideration of their interests, priorities, and the objectives of the grant request. Effectively tailor your message by:

>> Understanding the grant criteria

>> Highlighting the problem and solution

>> Focusing on impact

>> Sharing a compelling story.

>> Highlighting your team's expertise

>> Addressing potential challenges

>> Being clear and concise

>> Demonstrating sustainability

>> Tailoring to the audience

AI SPOTLIGHT

AI can help with all these points to increase your chances of making a compelling case for your project and securing the grant funding you need to bring your vision to life.

Nailing Your Presentation

When people hear the word *presentation*, their minds automatically shift to a slide presentation. A presentation doesn't necessarily mean a slide presentation. The type of presentation will depend on the preferences of the grant committee, the nature of your project, and/or your own strengths as a presenter. Here are some typical types of presentations:

>> Interactive

>> Multimedia

>> Peer review

>> Problem–solution

>> Storytelling

>> Videoconferencing

>> Slides or videos

>> Pitch to sell your idea

SHERYL SAYS

Take a look at the TV show *Shark Tank*. It's like a crash course in pitching ideas and selling visions. Entrepreneurs face the daunting task of articulating their concepts succinctly, highlighting their unique value proposition, and demonstrating market potential — all under the scrutiny of savvy investors. It's a masterclass in persuasion, where clarity, passion, and a solid business plan can turn a fledgling idea into a lucrative opportunity. Check out the nearby sidebar, "Daring to be different," for an example of how this can help you to win a grant.

DARING TO BE DIFFERENT

Carlo attended my presentation workshop. He was one of five finalists competing for a large research grant. Initially, he approached me with a stack of data-filled slides, hoping they would bolster his chances during his upcoming presentation. Seeing an opportunity for improvement, I challenged Carlo to rethink his approach. I painted a vivid scenario of the presentation day, urging him to consider how to keep the reviewers engaged amidst potentially dry presentations from his competitors. Drawing inspiration from the dynamic pitches seen on shows such as *Shark Tank*, I encouraged Carlo to abandon his slides in favor of a narrative-driven approach. I emphasized the importance of storytelling and crafting a memorable experience for the review panel, rather than overwhelming them with charts and graphs.

Initially hesitant, Carlo eventually embraced the challenge. He restructured his presentation to focus on storytelling, weaving together anecdotes of past successes and the broader impact of his research. Additionally, he meticulously prepared personalized handouts that highlighted key points to further illustrate his narrative. When the day of the presentations arrived, Carlo boldly took the stage as the first presenter. His approach resonated deeply with the grant reviewers who found his presentation refreshing and impactful. He set the bar very high.

Carlo's decision to prioritize storytelling and engagement proved to be a game-changer — he not only stood out, but he handily secured the grant! This solidified his reputation as a compelling communicator and strategic thinker. He was the hero.

Before your next presentation that you need to elevate from "Meh" to "Wow!" make sure you take a peek at my book, *Storytelling in Presentations For Dummies* (John Wiley & Sons, Inc., 2024). It's packed with tips for crafting captivating stories that will keep your reviewers hooked — just like Carlo did!

Preparing Slides Using AI Tools

AI SPOTLIGHT

Slide presentations are the most commonly sought after and the most commonly used types of presentations. They can be great for storytelling (check out Chapter 3). Remember that each slide is a canvas, awaiting the brushstrokes of clarity and insight. There are many helpful tools out there, and a few of the most popular are:

>> **AppleKeynote:** https://www.apple.com/keynote
>> **Canva:** https://www.canva.com
>> **Haiku Deck:** https://www.haikudeck.com
>> **PowerPoint:** https://www.microsoft.com/en-us/microsoft-365/powerpoint

>> **Slideshare:** `https://www.slideshare.net`

>> **Zoho Show:** `https://www.zoho.com/show`

REMEMBER

To avoid overwhelming your reviewers, focus on clear, concise, and meaningful visuals. Use engaging content and strategic pauses to maintain interest, prioritizing substance over style to create impactful presentations. Here are a few helpful do's and don'ts:

>> **Formatting do's for slides**

- Use a 24-point font for headlines and 18-point for text.
- Use upper and lower case, never all caps (even for the headline).
- Limit each visual to 5–7 lines of text.
- Use bulleted or numbered lists.
- Left-justify bullets and numbers.
- Limit bullets to one line of text when possible.
- Consider a *sans serif font* (such as Arial) for the headlines and a *serif font* (such as Times New Roman) for the text. Use black text on a light-colored background for the best readability.
- When using graphics and bullets on the same slide, place graphics either to left or right of the bulleted list.

>> **Formatting don'ts for slides**

- Avoid animation and sound effects (unless they're absolutely necessary). They're distractions.
- Avoid using italics (they decrease readability).
- Avoid the overuse of bullets with layers of sub-bullets.

Preparing Handouts That Leave a Lasting Impression

People like takeaways. If you've ever been to a tradeshow, you've witnessed how attendees grab literature, pens, pads, key chains, candy, and any other free gizmos on the tables. Most of these things get thrown away; the important things are kept and shared. Your review panel likes takeaways as well. They'll serve as memory refreshers after "Elvis has left the building." A handout is a wonderful way to add even more value to your presentation, regardless of the type you choose.

Making your handout shine

AI can help to add credence to your topic by locating articles, quotes, analogies, and other content, such as:

>> Success stories and testimonials

>> Simplified charts, tables, and diagrams

>> Case studies to show working examples of your mission

>> Relevant websites and blogs

>> Magazine, journal, and newspaper articles (with written permission from the publisher and/or author).

Be certain that each page displays your organization's name, contact information, and copyright notice. Attach your business card, and staple the handout about a half inch away from the edge of the paper, at a 45-degree angle on the left side. This positioning helps ensure visibility.

Including extras

You'll want the handout to extend beyond your presentation or to be given to reviewers who didn't attend. Kick your handout up a notch by including: lists; relevant content that's not in your presentation; references such as websites, blogs, articles, books, journals, and whitepapers; and anything else that will enhance the panel's experience.

Tools such as Microsoft Copilot (https://www.microsoft.com/en-us/microsoft-copilot) and Zapier https://zapier.com) can help with list management. And any of the popular chatbots will help you to find appropriate references.

Anticipating Questions

Anticipating questions from the review panel is crucial for preparing thorough and well-rounded responses during your presentation. You can effectively anticipate the panel's questions by:

>> Putting yourself in their shoes

>> Reviewing the proposal criteria

>> Thinking about potential concerns

>> Considering previous feedback

>> Researching previous grantees

>> Preparing responses in advance

By proactively anticipating questions from the review panel, you can better prepare yourself to respond effectively, demonstrate your expertise, and address any concerns they may have, ultimately increasing your chances of securing the grant funding.

**AI
SPOTLIGHT**

Tools such as ChatGPT (https://chatgpt.com) and Grammarly (http://www.grammarly.com) can analyze past review panel questions, identify common themes, and generate probable questions based on your content.

Practicing Your Way to Perfection

Rehearse your presentation multiple times to ensure that you're comfortable with the material and can deliver it confidently. Practice in front of a mirror, with colleagues, or record yourself to identify areas for improvement. Then, prepare for the big day by:

>> Gathering supporting materials

>> Making sure your technology is working properly

>> Dressing appropriately

>> Arriving early

>> Staying calm and confident

>> Wowing them!

AI tools such as VirtualSpeech (http://virtualspeech.com) and Orai (https://orai.com) can enhance your presentation by providing real-time feedback on delivery, helping to refine content, and simulating audience interactions to boost your confidence and effectiveness.

Be open to feedback. By demonstrating a receptive attitude and a willingness to engage with reviewers constructively, you position yourself as a thoughtful and collaborative researcher deserving of support and funding. This dialogue will build rapport, enhance your credibility, and increase your chances of success.

If you're ready to liberate your inner orator, try a private speaking coach with these AI tools:

>> **Gabble.ai:** https://gabble.ai

>> **Orai:** https://orai.com

>> **Verble:** https://www.verble.app

>> **Yoodli:** https://yoodli.ai

Following Up After Presenting

By following up after presenting, you demonstrate professionalism, responsiveness, and a genuine commitment to your research or project. These follow-up steps can help you maintain positive relationships with the panel members and increase your chances of success in securing funding for your work. Here are some suggestions for following up:

>> Send each member of the review panel a personalized thank you email or handwritten letter that expresses your gratitude for their time, attention, and valuable feedback. This demonstrates professionalism and appreciation for their efforts.

>> Connect with panel members on professional networking platforms such as LinkedIn and express your interest in staying in touch for future collaborations or opportunities.

Don't forget to let AI help. Here's an example of how it can assist with your follow-up message:

Prompt: *I need to send a 2-paragraph follow-up message to grant reviewers to thank them for allowing me to make my presentation for the grant. Cast this in a tone of enthusiasm to partner with them, and make it about them and not about me.*

AI's response:

Dear [Reviewers' Names],

Thank you for the opportunity to present my grant proposal on [date]. Your time and thoughtful feedback were greatly appreciated. The chance to engage with such a knowledgeable and dedicated team was truly valuable.

Looking forward to the possibility of collaborating and advancing this project together. Please let me know if there are any additional questions or information needed. Thanks again for your support and consideration!

Most sincerely,

[Your Name]

MOVING FORWARD WITH RENEWED FOCUS

Despite your best efforts, the proposal may be rejected. Perhaps competition was fierce, the budget or timeline were unrealistic, there were geopolitical or economic factors, or other valid reasons. Regardless the reason, it's like planning an elaborate surprise party for someone, putting in weeks of effort, and then the guest of honor is a no-show at the last minute. But instead of seeing rejection as a defeat, spin it like a compass pointing you toward unexpected adventures and renew your focus. Consider it a detour on the road to uncovering the pot of gold; after all, sometimes the most beautiful vistas are found off the beaten path.

Requesting feedback

Contact the funder. It's not just about understanding why the proposal didn't make the cut; it's about gathering insights to refine your approach, strengthening your weaknesses, and ultimately increasing your chances of reaching that coveted destination the next time. Embrace the feedback loop as a crucial part of the journey — a compass guiding you toward your pot of gold, even if it's hidden behind a few more bends in the road and if being guarded by a cunning leprechaun.

Asking questions

Here are examples of questions you can ask the funder (but don't overwhelm them with too many):

- Were the goals and objectives of the project clearly articulated?
- Were the methods and approach described in sufficient detail to understand how the project would be executed?
- How could the proposal be strengthened to better demonstrate its significance and innovation?
- Were there any methodological weaknesses or gaps in the proposed approach?
- Did the reviewers have any concerns about the budget allocation or justification?
- Were there any opportunities for additional collaborations or partnerships that were not addressed in the proposal?

If the funder doesn't respond, you can use the Freedom of Information Act (FOIA) after a proposal has been rejected by a government agency. This will get you the information you want, especially if you suspect unfairness or lack of transparency in the decision-making process. For more information visit http://www.foia.gov.

AI can come to your aid by analyzing feedback and identifying patterns in rejection reasons, suggesting targeted improvements, providing data-driven insights, and helping you refine your proposal to renew focus on key areas for a stronger resubmission.

5

The Part of Tens

Become a pitch-perfect pro and make sure your grant proposal hits every note, landing right in the sweet spot.

Understand why grant proposals flop so you can make yours not just sparkle, but shine like a beacon of brilliance.

Explore how AI can uncover funding treasures in the United States and globally, so you can glide smoothly toward the funding you need.

Chapter **14**

Ten Tips for Mastering the Tone of the Perfect Pitch

rafting a top-notch grant proposal is like suiting up for a big job interview. When your proposal shines, you're not just earning respect but also signaling the reviewers that you're serious about your game plan. Think of it as your moment to wow the reviewers. By mastering the perfect pitch through your tone, you're covering the bases and guaranteeing your pitch lands right in the strike zone for a grand-slam homer.

SHERYL SAYS

This chapter shows how AI can help can set the stage for your proposal's success. Striking the perfect balance in tone between writer intelligence (WI) and AI can turn heads, win hearts, and get funding.

Using AI as Your Assistant for the Proper Tone

The keyword here is "assistant." As a proposal writer, you play a vital role by infusing the proposal with stories, passion, confidence, and persuasiveness. In contrast, AI brings its analytical superpowers and wordsmithing. When combined harmoniously, the blend of WI and AI form a dynamic duo that elevates grant proposals to new heights of impact and success.

AI SPOTLIGHT

Check out these popular AI tools that can assist in turning those drab grant proposals into literary masterpieces that simply can't be ignored!

>> **Anyword:** https://anyword.com

>> **ChatGPT:** https://chatgpt.com

>> **Copy.ai:** https://www.copy.ai

>> **Grammarly:** https://app.grammarly.com

>> **Hemingway Editor:** https://hemingwayapp.com

>> **Jasper:** https://www.jasper.ai

>> **Notion:** https://www.notion.so

>> **QuillBot:** https://quillbot.com

>> **Rytr:** https://rytr.me

>> **Smart Copy:** https://www.smart-copy.io

>> **Writer:** https://ask.writer.com

>> **Writesonic:** https://writesonic.com

Shooting for Clarity

Tone plays a crucial role in achieving the clarity for a successful grant proposal. When you write with a tone that's straightforward and professional, you help ensure that your objectives, methods, and outcomes are communicated effectively. This clarity in tone aids in making your proposal more understandable and persuasive, allowing reviewers to easily grasp the significance and feasibility of your project.

A clear, confident tone also helps reviewers see how your project aligns with their priorities, enhancing the likelihood of a positive evaluation.

Expressing Passion

AI SPOTLIGHT

Passion demonstrates genuine commitment to the project adding authenticity by infusing it with authenticity and vigor. Prompt your chatbot to use words such as *wholehearted, vision, ardent, passion, enthusiast, revitalize, commitment, champion, catalyst, transformative, pioneering*, and others to express your strong enthusiasm.

Displaying Confidence

REMEMBER

Confidence in your project's feasibility and effectiveness assures reviewers of your organization's capability to achieve objectives, reflecting competence and professionalism through thorough research, planning, and requisite skills and resources for successful execution. It also shapes perceptions of risk, positioning a confident applicant as skilled in overcoming challenges and adapting to unforeseen circumstances.

AI SPOTLIGHT

Prompt your chatbot to use words such as *proven, determined, decisive, guarantee, expertise, robust, assure, capable, achieve, certain, confident*, and others to inspire trust in your ability to deliver results and enhance funding.

Using the Power of Persuasion

A persuasive tone crafts a narrative that informs and motivates reviewers to support the project. This strategically emphasizes its significance, feasibility, and potential impact, aiming to convince reviewers of its merit. Include compelling evidence such as stories, testimonials, statistics, or case studies to illustrate the merits of the proposal.

Prompt your chatbot to use words such as *compelling, critical need, vital, transformative, unprecedented opportunity,* and others that convey persuasion.

Maximizing Impact

Maximizing impact involves highlighting the potential benefits and outcomes of the proposed project, illustrating its potential to create positive change and address unmet needs within the target community or field. Through clear and compelling communication, a grant proposal can elevate reviewers' understanding and appreciation of the project's relevance and potential impact, increasing the likelihood of securing their support and funding.

Prompt your chatbot to include words such as *innovative, strategic, transformative, cost-effective,* and *sustainable.*

Expressing Gratitude

Gratitude conveys humility and professionalism, reflecting positively on the applicant's character and values. It also serves as a reminder of the impact that the funder's support can have, inspiring confidence in the potential success of the proposed project.

Prompt your chatbot to include words such as *grateful, support, recognition, valuable, honored, and thank you* that not only honor the funder's contribution but also strengthen the connection.

Maintaining a Positive Tone

A positive tone is crucial because it influences the funder's perception of your project and organization. It adds credibility and competence, passion and commitment, excitement and urgency. It fosters a personal connection.

Prompt your chatbot to include words such as *promising, robust, strategic, optimistic, proactive approach,* and *encouraging results.*

Using Industry-Related Jargon Sparingly and Appropriately

WARNING

Industry-related jargon refers to any specialized terms used within a particular field. This can be problematic if the proposal will be reviewed by people who aren't familiar with these terms.

Here's a solution: When using industry-specific terms, provide a brief explanation the first time you mention it, and thereafter use the abbreviation. For example:

> *Our proposal includes the integration of Application Programming Interfaces (APIs), which are tools that allow different software applications to communicate with each other.* (Thereafter you can use APIs.)

REMEMBER

If your proposal has a glossary, include any terms you think the reviewers may not be familiar with. Your entry may look like this:

> *API (Application Programming Interface): A set of rules and tools for building software applications, allowing different programs to interact with each other.*

Focusing on the Grantor

Focus on the grantor to increase your chances of securing funding for your project. Phrases such as *together we can . . .* suggest partnership and mutual support towards a common objective, not just a plea for funding.

Chapter **15**

Ten Reasons Why Grant Proposals May Fail

G etting funding may seem a bit like catching a fire-breathing dragon with a butterfly net! Perhaps you've been there. You craft what feels like the epitome of proposals, only to watch it disappear into the abyss of rejections. This chapter shares some reasons why grant proposals may fail. So grab your quill (or sit at your keyboard), and let's explore why, sometimes, even the most brilliant proposals don't get funded.

AI SPOTLIGHT

As you read this chapter, keep in mind that AI is far more than a mere tool — it's a transformative powerhouse. AI has the potential to revolutionize your processes, reveal crucial insights, and refine your decision-making. By harnessing its capabilities, you can significantly boost the effectiveness of your proposal, showcasing it as a beacon of innovation and excellence in your industry. Embrace AI to not only meet challenges head-on but to redefine what's possible in your proposal.

SHERYL SAYS

Want to see a masterpiece proposal in action? Check out Chapter 12!

Sending a Poorly Written Cover Letter

The cover letter acts as the trusty herald, announcing the arrival of your proposal to the majestic gates of the funding kingdom. Much like a knight's introduction before a joust, the cover letter sets the tone for the adventure that lies within. Whether you're submitting the proposal online, via email, or hard copy, the cover letter is the first impression. Uncover the nuances of the cover letter in Chapter 8 and learn how AI can help create a winner.

Presenting a Deficient Executive Summary

WARNING

In the world of grant proposals, the executive summary serves as a signpost — a beacon of hope for weary reviewers seeking clarity amidst a sea of words. A poorly written executive summary is like a foggy mirror, obscuring the brilliance of your proposal and leaving reviewers scratching their heads wondering, "Where's the beef?" Dive into Chapter 10 to learn how to help your executive summary capture the essence of your grant proposal with the aid of AI.

Lacking Innovation and Impact

Imagine being at a grand masquerade ball, surrounded by a sea of extravagant masks and dazzling costumes. In this whirlwind of creativity and imagination, you merely put on a funky hat. You stand out like a wilted flower in a field of vibrant blooms. Such is the fate of a grant proposal that lacks innovation. It's a drab shadow in a world of dazzling ideas.

REMEMBER

Innovation is the lifeblood that fuels progress and ignites the imagination. It can transform mundane projects into visionary quests, capturing the hearts and minds of reviewers like a mesmerizing enchantment.

Reviewers are wise sages, seeking proposals that dare to push the boundaries of knowledge and challenge the status quo. They look for projects that introduce new ideas or approaches. Proposals that fail to demonstrate innovation or fail to differentiate themselves from existing initiatives may struggle to stand out. Chapter 6 explores keywords that can add pizzazz to your grant proposal with the help of AI.

Presenting Inadequate Evidence of Making a Difference

WARNING

A proposal lacking evidence that it can make a difference is like a castle built on shifting sands — a grand vision without a solid foundation. In a world where resources are scarce and demands are many, reviewers are wary of empty promises and hollow claims. Funders want to see evidence that their investment will make a difference. Check out the Kick-Start Brief in Chapter 4 to highlight how you can make a difference and how AI can contribute.

Omitting to Express Partnership or Collaboration

Let the potential funder know you're looking to form a partnership, not just asking for funds. Expressions such as *together we can . . .* can be just what you need to raise your collaborative voice.

Include *letters of partnership* from other collaborators. This refers to other researchers, institutions, organizations, or entities that will contribute expertise, resources, or support to the project.

Presenting an Unrealistic Budget

An unrealistic budget is like a ship setting sail without a map — it's destined for trouble. Reviewers expect proposals to demonstrate a clear understanding of the costs involved and to align those costs with the proposed activities and outcomes. Include a detailed budget narrative that explains how each cost aligns with the project's objectives and timelines.

AI is very valuable here! It can do a cost analysis, align objectives, integrate a timeline, ensure consistency and accuracy, and even generate a table.

Sharing an Insufficient Evaluation Plan

An *evaluation plan* outlines how the project's effectiveness, outcomes, and processes will be measured and assessed. An inadequate evaluation plan signals a lack of foresight and accountability on the part of the applicant. Reviewers want to see that the project will be rigorously evaluated to ensure accountability and continuous improvement.

AI can help to prepare an evaluation plan to clearly outline measurable objectives, indicators, data collection methods, and analysis techniques.

Poorly Defining Goals and Objectives

Poorly defined goals can be the executioner's blade for a proposal, severing its chances of success with a single stroke. When goals are vague or undefined, it's like trying to hit a target with a blindfold on — you may aim, but you're unlikely to hit the mark. Reviewers crave clarity and direction; they want to know precisely what you aim to achieve and how you plan to get there. Without this clarity, your presentation lacks focus and purpose, wandering aimlessly through a maze of ideas and possibilities.

AI can help articulate goals and objectives by analyzing project details, specifying measurable statements aligned with overall objectives, and providing examples.

Missing the Mark

What can cause a proposal to miss the mark? Perhaps it lacks clarity, coherence, or conviction which undermines its credibility and fails to inspire confidence in the reviewers. Just like a poorly rehearsed play, a weakly presented proposal leaves the reviewer feeling disengaged and unconvinced.

Here's how AI can jump in not only to help you hit the mark, but to compel the reviewers to request an encore:

>> Reorganizing and refining the content for better structure and flow.

>> Suggesting ways to articulate ideas more compellingly and align with reviewers' expectations.

>> Creating polished and impactful visual elements that not only attract attention but ensure your message is delivered with clarity.

>> Pinpointing areas lacking detail or clarity.

>> Polishing the proposal like a finely cut diamond, making it sparkle with clarity and professionalism.

Not Using AI as a Writing Assistant

And last but certainly not least . . . not using AI as an assistant is akin to choosing to navigate a vast ocean without the aid of modern technology such as GPS!

By not using AI, you may be limiting your proposal in the following ways:

>> Missing opportunities for data analysis.

>> Limiting efficiency in literature review.

>> Reducing precision in predictive modeling.

>> Limiting accessibility, collaboration, and resources.

>> Decreasing competitiveness in review process.

>> Reducing adaptability to evolving conditions.

>> Overlooking alternative approaches.

>> Restricting ability to incorporate stakeholder feedback.

Chapter **16**

Ten Ways to Find Funding in the United States and Globally

Pursuing grant money is much like pursuing leprechauns and their pots of gold. Both embody a quest for something valuable and often elusive. Both quests are fraught with challenges, uncertainties, and the need for strategic planning. Leprechauns, with their elusive nature and penchant for trickery, can be likened to the unpredictable landscape of funding. Grant writers must navigate through a maze of guidelines, requirements, and competition, using strategic thinking and creativity to capture the attention of funders.

SHERYL SAYS

This chapter offers a glimpse into some of the available funding opportunities in the United States, United Kingdom, Canada, and Australia and how AI can assist. For a more comprehensive guide to funding, consult *Grant Writing For Dummies,* 7th edition by Dr. Beverly A. Browning (John Wiley & Sons, Inc., 2022). And there's more:

>> Crowdfunding sites such as Kickstarter (https://www.kickstarter.com) and GoFundMe (https://www.gofundme.com) can offer assistance.

>> Networks such as LinkedIn (https://www.linkedin.com) can connect you with potential donors or funders.

Harnessing the Power of AI

By harnessing the power of AI, you can navigate the complex landscape of grant funding more effectively, ultimately increasing your chances of securing the financial support you need. AI can automate the search process, send you ongoing alerts, provide automatic filtering, understand and analyze grants, personalize assistance, and more. Here are a few places to start:

>> **Granter.ai** (https://granter.ai) allows you to create an account effortlessly. Start by providing some basic information about your business, and they'll match you with opportunities.

>> **OpenGrants** (https://www.opengrants.io) offers a comprehensive database of over 5,000 active grants throughout the United States The database is updated weekly and, with the magic of AI, they can match grant funders with your organization's profile.

>> **The Grant Portal** (https://www.thegrantportal.com) is one of the largest online grant catalogs with loads of grants you can view.

Learning of Direct Grant Opportunities

Direct grants in the United States can come from various sources, including government agencies, private foundations, corporations, and nonprofit organizations. These sites often walk you through the process of applying or give you contact information. Here are some opportunities for direct grants:

>> **Federal government:** The United States federal government offers a wide range of grants to support various initiatives, including scientific research, education, healthcare, community development, and social services.

- >> **State governments:** Each state has its own grant programs to support local initiatives, economic development, infrastructure projects, education, healthcare, and other programs.

- >> **Local governments:** These include cities, counties, and municipalities that offer grants to support community development, public infrastructure, social services, arts and culture, and similar local initiatives.

- >> **Private foundations:** Many private foundations in the United States offer grants to support charitable causes and initiatives aligned with their mission and funding priorities. Some well-known foundations include the Bill & Melinda Gates Foundation, Ford Foundation, Rockefeller Foundation, and Pew Charitable Trusts.

- >> **Nonprofit organizations:** Many charitable foundations and community organizations offer grants to support projects and programs that align with their mission and objectives. These grants may be targeted towards specific geographic areas, populations, or issues.

To access federal, state, and local funding, start by identifying relevant grants and programs through official government websites, such as www.grants.gov for federal funding. Research state-specific resources via your state's government website or economic development office. For local funding, check with city or county offices, community foundations, and local business development agencies.

Finding Pass-Through Grant Opportunities

Pass-through grants, also known as fiscal sponsorship grants, are funds given by a donor to a sponsoring organization, which then distributes the funds to another organization or individual to carry out specific activities. This may include community foundations, nonprofit intermediaries, donor-advised funds (DAFs), public charitable and umbrella organizations, and philanthropic collaboratives, which are partnerships between multiple organizations or individuals working together to address social issues, pool resources, and leverage collective expertise for greater impact.

Tapping into the Small Business Innovation Research (SBIR) Program

The SBIR program is a federal initiative aimed at stimulating technological innovation by funding small businesses' research and development efforts. Managed by the United States Small Business Administration (SBA), SBIR grants are awarded in phases, beginning with feasibility studies and potentially progressing to full-scale development. Participating federal agencies, such as NASA, National Institute of Health (NIH), and the Department of Defense (DOD), and others issue specific solicitations aligned with their research priorities. To find out more, visit (https://www.sbir.gov).

Funding for Nonprofits

REMEMBER

There are estimated to be 1.97 million nonprofits currently operating in the United States and funding can make the difference between thriving, surviving, or folding. And that doesn't count the 1.48 million 501(c)(3) tax exempt organizations. Here are some examples:

>> Grant databases and search engines

>> Foundation website

>> Government agencies

>> Professional associations and networks

>> Subscription services and newsletters

>> Networking and collaborative

>> Local community foundations

>> Corporate giving programs

Two great resources for nonprofits are GrantStation (https://grantstation.com) and GrantWatch https://www.grantwatch.com).

Funding for a Wide Variety of Industries

REMEMBER

Across diverse fields such as education, healthcare and biotech, agriculture and environmental conservation, arts and culture, energy and sustainability, and social enterprise and impact investing, a unifying theme emerges in their pursuit of funding opportunities. Each sector taps into a wide array of funding sources, including grants, scholarships, venture capital, government programs, and support from nonprofit organizations.

This diverse funding landscape allows initiatives to secure financial backing tailored to their specific needs and developmental stages, whether through *seed funding* (startups or early-stage projects) for innovative biotech research or grants supporting cultural preservation projects.

Moreover, these sectors share a commitment to addressing sector-specific challenges and opportunities, ensuring that funding initiatives are tightly aligned with their respective missions. Whether advancing medical breakthroughs in biotech, promoting sustainable farming practices in agriculture, or fostering creativity and cultural heritage in arts and culture, the focus remains on driving positive impact and fostering innovation.

To find funding for specific industries, research industry-specific grants, venture capital firms, and angel investors who focus on that sector. Attend industry conferences, network with professionals, and explore government and nonprofit funding programs tailored to your field.

Going Global

Accessing global funding can be a game-changer for initiatives aiming to make a significant impact on an international scale. With a wealth of opportunities available through international grants, investments, and philanthropic efforts, navigating this complex landscape requires a strategic approach.

Understanding global funding sources, from multilateral organizations and international foundations to venture capital firms and government grants, and crafting a compelling proposal can unlock the resources needed to drive meaningful change and achieve your project's objectives on a global stage.

Many of these sources use AI to offer global funding opportunities.

>> Online platforms such as GrantWatch and FundsforNGOs (https://www.fundsforngos.org) provide global funding opportunities.

>> Government and NGO websites such as the United Nations, World Bank, and International Monetary Fund offer global funding for various projects.

>> Philanthropic organizations such as the Bill & Melinda Gates Foundation (https://www.gatesfoundation.org) are great resources.

>> Open society foundations (https://www.opensociety foundations.org) provide funding for projects worldwide.

And this is where humans come in. Don't overlook the following which you can find with an online search:

>> **Conferences and webinars:** International conferences and webinars often feature global funding opportunities and attract representatives from funding agencies around the world.

>> **Professional networks:** Global professional networks and associations frequently share information about international funding opportunities.

>> **Newsletters:** Many global funding bodies and international foundations provide newsletters with updates on worldwide funding opportunities.

Securing Funding in the United Kingdom

Approximately 168,000 registered charities exist in the United Kingdom, though this number fluctuates due to new registrations, closures, or changes in status. These nonprofits access funding through various channels including grants, donations, sponsorships, events, membership fees, social enterprises, legacy giving, crowdfunding, trusts, foundations, and government contracts, each tailored to their specific activities and goals.

By leveraging AI tools, charities can better match their needs with suitable funding sources, improve efficiency in managing dona-tions, and gain insights into donor behavior and preferences. For example, AI can help organizations navigate funding oppor-tunities from United Kingdom Research and Innovation (UKRI), The Wellcome Trust, Arts Council England, The National Lottery Community Fund, and the Heritage Lottery Fund, ensuring they maximize their chances of securing support.

Finding Funding in Canada

Grant opportunities in Canada, reflecting its vast landscapes and cultural diversity, support approximately 170,000 nonprofits. Government grants from federal to municipal levels, research funding and resources to bolster arts, culture, business innova-tion, and various sectors including social services, environmental conservation, education, and healthcare. Municipalities, commu-nity organizations, foundations, corporations, and educational grants further enrich this supportive ecosystem.

Ask AI for more information on the Natural Sciences and Engi-neering Research Council of Canada (NSERC), Social Sciences and Humanities Research Council of Canada (SSHRC), Canadian Insti-tutes of Health Research (CIHR), Canada Foundation for Inno-vation (CFI), Canada Council for the Arts, Canadian Heritage, and Mitacs.

Navigating Funding Opportunities in Australia

Australia's dynamic nonprofit sector, comprising about 600,000 organizations, offers diverse funding opportunities including government grants, philanthropic support from foundations like The Ian Potter Foundation and The Myer Foundation, corporate sponsorships, community grants, crowdfunding platforms, and international grants. It's essential to grasp eligibility criteria, deadlines, and cultivate strong funder relationships to sustain impactful initiatives.

AI can make your search for funding opportunities much smoother. It can quickly match your charity's needs with the right sources from organizations that offer funding like the Australian Research Council (ARC) or the National Health and Medical Research Council (NHMRC). It also helps streamline your applications and provides insights into trends from places like the Australian Council for the Arts and the Australian Renewable Energy Agency (ARENA). In short, AI takes the guesswork out of finding and applying for grants, making the whole process a lot easier and more effective.

Index

S

Y

Z

About the Author

Sheryl Lindsell-Roberts, a transplanted New Yorker living in Boston, has a distinctive NY accent that bears testament to her roots (as she charmingly says, "cough-ee"). She's carved an illustrious career path fueled by her mastery of words. Raised by a grammar-obsessed mother who introduced her to complex vocabulary at the age of five, Sheryl's early fascination with language evolved into a lifelong passion and career. Armed with a Master's Degree in Business and English, she founded her own communications firm Sheryl Lindsell-Roberts & Associates.

Sheryl is known for her ability to synthesize crucial information into impactful content, making her a sought-after workshop facilitator and business communications expert. Her influence reaches far and wide, reflected in a prolific bibliography of over 25 books spanning the genres of business writing and humor. Notably, her proposals have secured millions of dollars in grant funding for numerous companies, highlighting her strategic acumen, storytelling prowess, and persuasive writing talent. Sheryl is an ongoing contributor to *Training* magazine and has been featured in *The New York Times, Entrepreneur, Inc.,* and other publications.

Beyond her professional achievements, Sheryl embraces creative pursuits, from interior decorating and poetry to outdoor adventures such as kayaking and cross-country skiing. She finds inspiration in gardening, painting (pictures not walls), yoga, playing the violin, exploring the world and, most of all, spending time with family.

Sheryl remains a beacon in the communications landscape, leaving her indelible mark on a wide variety of industries. To learn more, visit Sheryl on LinkedIn at www.linkedin.com/in/sherylwrites.

(By the way, the draft of this spirited bio was crafted by ChatGPT with the help of prompts Sheryl provided. With her writer intelligence [WI], she further brought this bio to life.)

Dedication

To my mother, my guiding light and master of words. I can never thank her enough for the priceless lessons she instilled in me. From the time I could talk she made sure I spoke clearly and articulately, even if it meant endless hours of pronunciation practice. Her unwavering faith in the transformative power of language has molded me into the person I am today and guided me towards varied professions where communication reigns supreme. Whether I'm leading workshops, captivating audiences with my public-speaking skills, tackling writing projects, or simply engaging in everyday conversations, I carry her cherished teachings with me.

Author's Acknowledgments

Here's to the return of the Fab Four — the literary Beatles. Writing a book is like composing a symphony: It wouldn't be complete without the talented people who fine-tuned each note along the way. I'd like to acknowledge each one in order of appearance:

>> **Me,** the Author, for hatching this concept and laying down the foundation — adopting the role of the visionary and wordsmith, much like Sir Paul on bass.

>> **Tracy Boggier,** Acquisitions Editor, who deserves a huge shout-out for bringing this vision to life, working behind the scenes to make it happen, much like George did with his thoughtful guitar solos.

>> **Dan Mersey,** Development Editor, has been the maestro behind the scenes, orchestrating the flow and rhythm of each chapter — channeling John's lyrical brilliance with every edit. (Like John, Dan is from the United Kingdom and plays a great guitar riff.)

>> **Meir Zimmerman,** Technical Editor, provided the essential behind-the-scenes review, ensuring every technical detail sings true — reminiscent of Ringo's steady beat that holds it all together.

Together, this team rock 'n rolled from concept through drafts and revisions, striving for perfection with the determination of the Fab Four themselves. This was truly a magical journey.

Publisher's Acknowledgments

Acquisitions Editor: Tracy Boggier
Development Editor: Dan Mersey
Technical Editor: Meir Zimmerman

Managing Editor: Sofia Malik
Cover Image: © Nichcha/ Shutterstock